Brothers Born
of Adversity

How the Bonds of Friendship Helped Two Men
Survive the Horrors of Japanese Prison Camps
and the Infamous Hell Ships During WWII

By Larry Dean Reese

Cover Photo: George Crowell being surprised to find his two army nurse sisters waiting for him upon his arrival in Okinawa after spending over 44 months in Japanese prison camps.

Dedication

Dedicated to all our military veterans and
their families who sacrificed greatly for the freedom
we enjoy today and to

Martin A. Schneider
(1951-2020)

A great friend who was like a brother,
and who brought much joy and laughter to many.

Endorsements

"Brothers Born of Adversity is a story of two men, George W. Crowell and Frank "Max" Maxwell, both US Navy Corpsmen who became friends while held by the Japanese. . . What is important in this study of these two individuals is their bond which forces them to survive the harsh atrocities inflicted on them by the Japanese which in a number of cases most men did not. . . The book is more than just a story of what happened to two POWs during World War II. It is a story of two lives and how they lived during a period in American history that was not the best of times. Yet it tells the story of these two men who became part of the great generation, who stood up for democracy, who did their duty and went on to be successful in their civilian lives, having families and maintaining a close relationship based on what they experienced as a POW; a story worth reading."

----James S. Brockman, Petty Officer 2nd Class (Ret) U.S. Navy. Executive Director, National American Defenders of Bataan and Corregidor Museum and Research Center

"This is a horrific episode from WWII that should not be forgotten. The author has masterfully woven the ordeal of two navy corpsmen held by the Japanese and how their bond of friendship helped them beat the odds to survive years of brutal imprisonment. The story is more than a historical war event that describes some of the worst in human nature. But it is also a story of friendship, family, faith, and factors that may have helped them survive, as well as to live rather normal lives after experiencing such harrowing events."

----Joy Neal Kidney, Author of *Leora's Dexter Stories* and *Leora's Letters*

"This is a great book that tells the stories of two heroes that were a part of our country's greatest generation. I know that both their families must be proud to be a part of their history."

----Mark Oglesby, Sergeant Major (Ret) U.S. Army. Director of Legislative Affairs for the Florida Department of Military Affairs

"Brothers Born of Adversity is a powerful example and reminder of the importance of relationships in overcoming adversity. This book made me more thankful for my relationships; with friends, with family, with Christ."

----Billy Francis, Colonel (Ret) U.S. Air Force. Director, Student Veterans Center, Florida State University

"Larry Reese has written a wonderful book that takes a look at the experiences of the individual on the ground rather than the admirals and generals at the top. We know about MacArthur, Chesty Puller and Admiral Nimitz. Mr. Reese gives us a heartfelt look at two individuals brought together by war at its most challenging. Spending time as a Prisoner of War can never be considered as anything but devastating to the human spirit. The support that George Wyman Crowell and Frank "Max" Maxwell provided each other during their captivity helped them survive. The experience also laid the groundwork for a lifetime friendship created by mutual suffering. Brothers Born of Adversity is a well told account of adapting and overcoming circumstances that confront human beings on the front line of war. Highly recommended."

----Daniel J. McDonald, Lt. Col. (Ret) U.S. Army

"This story represents a part of the Pacific War during World War II that is too often neglected or overlooked. The perseverance and survival of these two Navy corpsmen in the face of the most brutal, horrifying conditions and abuse is remarkable. The inhumanity of man upon man cannot be overstated in this story. Many Americans today would be well served to read this book and become more fully informed of the sacrifices of their forebears in providing the freedoms they enjoy today."

---- Les Akers, Retired businessman and lifelong history enthusiast with a special interest and study of all things involving World War II

Brothers Born of Adversity:
How the Bonds of Friendship Helped Two Men Survive the Horrors of Japanese Prison Camps and the Infamous Hell Ships During WWII

By Larry Dean Reese

A friend loveth at all times, and a brother is born for adversity.
Proverbs 17:17 KJV

George Wyman Crowell   Frank "Max" L. Maxwell

"Of all the cases of brutality and mistreatment accorded prisoners of war that have come out of World War II, none can compare with the torment and torture suffered by our soldiers, who were prisoners of war of the Japanese, aboard the ships, Oryoku Maru, Brazil Maru and Enoura Maru on the voyage from Manila to Japan during the months of December 1944 and January 1945. It is a saga of men driven to madness by sadistic and sensual captors. Today, of the 1619 men who set sail on the voyage, less than 200 are alive. I have read diaries, written at the time, tomes of recorded testimony, have talked to survivors, and no place in recorded history can one find anything so gruesome and horrible. No mitigating circumstances can explain or condone such cruelty. The callous and vile conduct of the captors will live in infamy!"

The above statement was made by Mr. Alva C. Carpenter, Chief Legal Section, General Headquarters, Supreme Commander for the Allied Powers, during the war crimes trial of those responsible for the deaths and cruel and inhumane treatment of the POWs. See Appendix A for entire summary.

Brothers Born of Adversity

Table of Contents

Brothers Born of Adversity

Preface

I thought it might be useful to begin with how I came to write this book. I have known George Crowell's son, Perry, for around 30 years. We were colleagues at Florida State University and over the years became close friends. Occasionally, Perry would mention that his father was a prisoner of war during WWII. I love history and believe family history should be preserved and had often encouraged him to research and write a book about his father's life and war experiences. In doing so it would be preserved for his children, grandchildren, and others who have an interest in history.

Since I had some experience writing and publishing two books about my own family history, Perry suggested that I should consider writing such a book. Perry and his wife, Marilyn, had been very helpful in editing one of my earlier books, so I knew that they would be a great help if I decided to take on this project. With the onset of the Covid-19 pandemic in early 2020 and the need to stay closer to home, it seemed like a good time to take up the project to research and write his father's story.

After starting my research, I realized that it would be difficult to tell George's story without including the story of George's close friend, Frank "Max" Maxwell. The two men had become close friends while prisoners of the Japanese and learned to rely on each other in the midst of severe adversity; to the point where they became as close as brothers. While I found their story fascinating, telling it was not without its challenges. Both men had passed away years earlier and had not shared much of the details of their imprisonment with their families. As a result, it was necessary to piece together their story from the few recollections that their families had of what they'd been told, as well as from various documents that George and Max had left and other available books and material about the events they experienced.

In addition to spending years in Japanese prison camps in the Philippines and Japan, George and Max also managed to survive transport from the Philippines to Japan on what became known as the infamous hell ships. In their case only one out of six of those being transported would live to see the end of the war. While there were a

1

Brothers Born of Adversity

number of these Japanese transport ships that were referred to as hell ships, as a result of their deplorable conditions, George and Max's journey on the *Oryoku Maru*, *Enoura Maru*, and *Brazil Maru* was the best documented, and therefore made their story much easier to research.

It is my hope that this book will do justice in telling and preserving the story of the horrific events that they and the other POWs experienced.

----Larry Dean Reese

Brothers Born of Adversity

Foreword

We all have a story to tell. Some of our stories are difficult to put into words but have made everlasting impressions on who we are as a person. The story of my father, George Wyman Crowell, should not go unrecognized or be forgotten. It has taken me over 60 years to come to this conclusion.

There is no question that my father lived through experiences much worse than I or most anyone can conceive, serving his country during WWII. His story is quite remarkable and you will find yourself wondering how a human being could endure and survive the brutality and deprivation of being a prisoner of war of the Japanese. You will read about these experiences in this book and can judge for yourself.

My childhood experiences did not mirror what I watched on TV growing up in the late 1950s and 1960s; shows like Family Affair, Father Knows Best, and Leave it to Beaver portrayed loving families experiencing the American dream. My guess is that for many families of veterans in United States during that time period, life was a constant struggle that included emotional, physical, and financial challenges.

Growing up, my relationship with my father was not a close one. With the benefit of hindsight, I believe he must have been suffering from Post-Traumatic Stress Disorder (PTSD) and possibly physical complaints resulting from his time in captivity. PTSD was not well understood or treated at that time, and he certainly didn't seek out or receive therapy. Additionally, many veterans, including my father, rarely talked about their wartime experiences. For all these reasons, plus the fact of my youth and lack of awareness, we did not connect. Sadly, I lost my father in 1982 when I was in my late 20's, long before I would become curious about his wartime experiences and how they affected his life, and ultimately, mine.

I am greatly indebted to my good friend, Larry Reese, for encouraging me to learn more about my father's war experiences. He took an interest in my father's story and ultimately offered to research and write it for publication. Larry has spent countless hours researching and documenting the details of my father's life, military history, and wartime experiences. Without his efforts, this story would have been lost for future generations to better understand what our veterans and their families sacrificed to achieve and preserve our freedom. It is an important part of American history.

By exploring the factors that shaped my father's life, and reflecting on my relationship with him, I now have a better understanding of who my father was and appreciate and admire the man who endured years of brutal imprisonment and suffered greatly for our country.

-----Perry Wyman Crowell

Brothers Born of Adversity

Acknowledgements

First, let me begin by recognizing that I would not have been able to effectively research and write this story without the help of George's son, Perry Crowell and his wife, Marilyn Crowell, who were so helpful in assisting with researching and editing this work. Perry's cousins, Quentin A. Humberd, Michele Maxwell Galan, George Gary Maxwell, and Brenda Humberd Tatum were also very generous with their time and incredibly helpful with the stories, photos, and information they shared. During a visit to the town of Berry, Alabama, Mayor Jimmy Madison graciously met with Perry and me and shared the history of the town where George and his sisters grew up. Pat Hunt, Janine Welch, Ron and Linda Chastain, Skip Owen, Daniel J. McDonald, Anthony B. McDonald, and Les Akers gave freely of their time and talents in providing additional editing. Author, Joy Neal Kidney, offered helpful suggestions. Larry Walker helped with editing and formatting the final draft to meet publishing requirements.

Perry and I were also able to meet with James Brockman, Executive Director of the National American Defenders of Bataan and Corregidor Museum and Research Center in Wellsburg, WV, Dr. Richard Lizza, Board President, and interns Chloe Cross and Marya Squire. They provided resources, feedback, and helped verify the historical accuracy of the story from a military perspective. Their expertise and vast collection of relevant materials is a must use resource for any serious researcher of the events relating to the battles of Bataan and Corregidor, the imprisonment of POWs in the Philippines, and the hell ship experiences. In addition, Bridget Beers, Curator of the National Prisoner of War Museum in Andersonville, Georgia provided several leads that were helpful in the development of this manuscript. Senator Marco Rubio and staff assisted with obtaining George Crowell's military service records.

Other individuals who provided valuable assistance include:
- Linda Dahl Weeks, who maintains the website for WWII Japanese POW Fukuoka Camp # 17.
- Dr. G. Kurt Piehler, Director of the Institute on World War II and the Human Experience and Associate Professor of History at Florida State University.

5

Brothers Born of Adversity

- Wes Injerd, who maintains the website for the Center for Research, Allied POWs Under the Japanese.
- Bob Whitecotton, moderator for the Japanese-POW Listserv and webmaster for the Japanese-POW website.

It is also important to recognize that this book would not have been possible if many of the survivors had not told their stories. In the bibliography I have listed a number of publications and other sources that I used in my research and which allowed me to put together the story of George and Max's prisoner of war experience. I am thankful for having these great resources to use in constructing their story.

I found the published sources to generally be consistent and complementary to the overall story, however, as one might expect from people recounting such experiences from memory and often years later, a number of the details were inconsistent. A few examples include inconsistent dates of events, counts of survivors, food provided, whether they had straw or cotton mats, etc. These differences were not substantive to the overall story but did necessitate me making decisions as to which might be the most accurate to use for this book. Not one of the books or other materials i used told the complete same story of George and Max's POW experiences, although there were definitely experiences that overlapped at times. By relying on the sources where the overlapping experiences occurred, I was able to piece together a fairly complete story of their prisoner of war experiences, although many details of their treatment will never be fully known.

Brothers Born of Adversity

Introduction

This is the true account of two navy corpsmen from Alabama, George Wyman Crowell and Frank "Max" Maxwell. These two men served our country during WWII and found themselves, again and again, in horrific, cruel, and unimaginable circumstances as prisoners of war (POWs) of the Japanese Empire for 44 and 40 months respectively. George and Max had become close friends while imprisoned in the Philippines at the Bilibid Prison in Manila. While internment at Bilibid was atrocious, they had no idea of the extent of the horrors that they were to experience over a seven-week period while being transported on what would become the most documented of the so-called hell ship voyages.

By December 1944, American forces had begun their invasion to liberate the Philippines from the Japanese Empire. Thousands of American and Allied military personnel had been captured by the Japanese nearly three years earlier, shortly after the start of WWII in the Pacific. Most of the POWs who had been held by the Japanese in the Philippines had already been shipped out to Japan, China, or Korea to be used as slave laborers in support of Japan's war effort. The POWs transported by the Japanese were often placed in overcrowded ship holds where men would suffer or die from lack of air, as well as limited food and water, disease, and abuse. Furthermore, these unmarked ships were often the target of American submarines and aircraft, who were not aware that the ships were transporting POWs. Due to their notoriety, these transport ships were often referred to as hell ships or death ships.

On the morning of December 13, 1944, 1,619 POWs were marched from the Bilibid prison to an awaiting ship named the *Oryoku Maru* for transport to Japan. On the subsequent voyage, George, Max, and their fellow prisoners had to not only survive the horrific conditions and treatment from their captors, but also the torpedoes, bombings, and strafing from American aircraft and submarines. In addition, they suffered from disease and at times even abuse from fellow POWs. Only one in six of those boarding the *Oryoku Maru* that day would live to see the end of the war and to return home.

Brothers Born of Adversity

Throughout such terrible experiences, George and Max had to maintain the strength and desire to survive. Many times, a word of encouragement shared between them in their darkest moments meant the difference between giving up and the determination to make it through another day. Family lore has it that George would often encourage Max by telling him of his five beautiful sisters that he wanted Max to meet after the war. Two of George's sisters had already become army nurses and, unknown to George, volunteered for duty in the Pacific Theater putting themselves in harm's way in hopes of finding their brother.

It is hoped that their story will be a tribute to not only George and Max, but to all those who gave and suffered for democracy, freedom from tyranny, and love of country.

Brothers Born of Adversity

Chapter 1 - The Early Years Before the War

George and his family lived only about 60 miles from where Max grew up, but there were as many differences in their lives and circumstances growing up as there were similarities. George was born on January 29, 1912, while Max was born seven and a half years later on August 25, 1919. Both grew up during the Great Depression era and in a similar southern culture. George's hometown was Berry, Alabama and Max's hometown was the city of Birmingham, Alabama. Both are in Central Alabama, but the terrain is different. The small town of Berry is considered part of the large coastal plain area that extends up from the Gulf of Mexico. The area has rolling hills, much of it in forests, with significant agricultural development. The Birmingham area is much hillier and is part of the foothills of the Appalachian Mountain range. Iron ore, coal, and limestone deposits in the Birmingham area allowed the city of Birmingham to become a major urban area and industrial hub, while the town of Berry only had a couple hundred residents and remained primarily a timber and agricultural community.

To better understand George and Max and what might have contributed to helping them survive their later ordeal as POWs, it was useful to look at their family relationships and their years growing up. Although their family relationships and experiences growing up were quite different in many ways, they did share having loving family relationships, a strong sense of values, belief in themselves, their country, and faith in God.

George was the second child and only son among six children born to Perry Allen Crowell (1886-1957) and Dovie Dunn Crowell (1889-1962). A listing of George and his sisters follows in their birth order:

Thelma ----------------------------- November 19, 1910
George Wyman-------------------- January 29, 1912
Aller Mae -------------------------- April 25, 1914
Imogene (known as Gene)------ February 27, 1921
Willie Nell-------------------------- March 2, 1924
Billie Dove ------------------------- April 7, 1928

Brothers Born of Adversity

George's grandfather, William Campbell Crowell, was born in Southern Illinois, but the family line goes back to North Carolina, and to a Peter Crowell (Croul) who arrived in Philadelphia from Germany on November 25, 1740, on the ship named "*Loyal Judith.*" A generation earlier, many German immigrants settled in New York, Pennsylvania, and the Carolinas, and were followed by thousands of new German immigrants searching for a better life for themselves and their children, more religious freedom, and an opportunity to be landowners.

George's mother's family, the Dunns and Bagwells, had deep roots in the Berry area, going back several generations, resulting in a large extended family of aunts, uncles, and cousins.

George's parents, Perry Allen and Dovie Crowell

George's father, Perry, was a very tall man – at least six foot six. He did some farming but worked primarily as a blacksmith. Being a blacksmith was an important skill set needed in the local community in the early 20th century. Blacksmiths not only shod horses but were important in repairing or forging agricultural equipment and other metal instruments needed in the community. Growing up, George would have been familiar with the sound of metal being hammered and the smell of burning charcoal used to heat metal.

In 1913, Perry and Dovie sold a 40-acre parcel of land and in 1917 they sold an additional 40 acres of land. Since cotton was the primary agricultural crop at the time, they were very likely impacted by the boll weevil infestation that destroyed much of the cotton crops in Alabama in the early 20th century. This may be the reason that they sold their farmland. Such events made life in the rural south difficult, which was made worse by the Great Depression that began in 1929 and lasted up until the start of WWII.

Supporting a wife and six children on what Perry made as a blacksmith and farming required him to work long hours. Although they did not have a lot of money, they had a close loving family relationship. Since they were able to grow most of their own food, they did not go hungry or have to wait in long bread lines during the Depression era like many of the poor and unemployed in the larger cities.

Perry was a quiet and reserved man - loving, but not one to show much affection. He was not a very religious person, at least not outwardly, and seemed to stay focused on his work and caring for the needs of his family. In later years, George would start showing more of these same traits. Dovie, on the other hand, was very open about her Christian faith and would make sure all the children attended church with her. While she was described as strict, she was also very loving and affectionate toward her children and in later years, her grandchildren. She was also very talkative, a trait that all the daughters seemed to inherit, and which made family conversations seem like a competition. This occasionally caused the daughters to get upset with one another, but they were generally quick to make amends.

During the earlier days as George and his sisters were growing up, the town of Berry had no paved streets, but it did have a bank, a drug store where one could also buy bus tickets, a railroad depot, a small city hall with a jail cell, a gas station, schools, and two mercantile stores. One of

Brothers Born of Adversity

the stores was Shephard's Mercantile and the other was Theron Cannon and Company, whose motto was, "Everything from a cradle to a coffin." The town also had several churches and, from 1912 to 1922, a small Christian college operated there.

Being the only son, George recognized that he was often "petted" by his parents and sisters and allowed to get away with some of his impulsive and mischievous ways. Once, while he was quite young, his father came home with a wagon load of hay and had left the wagon and mules still hitched and standing in the yard. George managed to climb up in the wagon and yell, "giddy-up!" as he had seen and heard his father do many times. The mules did not hesitate and quickly sped down the road with little George sitting in the wagon until he bounced out. George's father quickly ran to the barn and mounted a horse to chase down the runaway team of mules and wagon, which he finally managed to stop and turn back toward home. On the way back home, he stopped to pick up George, who somehow managed to not get hurt from his fall. While George may have learned a lesson about driving a team of mules that day, it did not do much to change his mischievous behavior.

In school, George would occasionally get into mischief and would routinely get "whippings" by his teachers. His parents would tell him that the kids he was hanging around with were a bad influence on him but it's possible the other kids' parents may have said the same thing about him. He would sometimes play hooky from school with his buddies and then tell his teachers he was either sick or had to work with his father. However, the truth would often come out later when the teachers talked to his parents. Despite George's interest in having a good time with his friends, he recognized the importance of schooling and, when he wanted to, he would study hard to keep from failing in school.

George's favorite time of year was summer when school was not in session and he could spend time out in the country with his cousins who lived near Windham Springs. The springs was an artesian well, which spouted out mineral or sulfur water. The well had been marketed as having health benefits and a hotel was built there to accommodate the many tourists who came for the supposed healing benefits of the water. When George was quite small a tornado came through the area and destroyed the hotel, but the springs remained popular with the locals who would come there to picnic and drink the water. George affectionately remembered the family having picnics there where they would enjoy homemade ice cream, cakes, and fruits.

Down the hill from the artesian well was a creek where he and his friends and cousins would often go swimming; sometimes until nearly dark. Perry and Dovie, like most parents, worried that George might drown and would always caution him to be careful. Often in the evening, George and his cousins would take a flashlight and go possum hunting and bird thrashing in the dark, but mostly it was just to play and have fun. Sometimes the child with the flashlight would turn the light off and leave the rest of the group in the dark for a while. This would create a bit of a frenzy, with screams and laughter all around. During his years of imprisonment as a POW, George would share stories with Max of those carefree days when he was young and his biggest concern was summer ending and having to start back to school.

During high school, one of George's teachers played a silent picture show titled, "Ham and Bud," about a comical pair of mischievous young men. George's classmates noted that George favored the character "Bud" and from then on George was proud to be known as "Bud," although his family referred to him by his middle name, Wyman.

As George grew older, his father expected him to play a greater role in helping with the chores around the home place and at his shop. However, George was more interested in playing ball and doing things with his friends. This caused a strain in the relationship between George and his father, who would give him harsh whippings for not doing his chores. Often his sisters would do the chores for George to keep him from getting another beating.

George seemed to be happy-go-lucky, not caring much for authority, and willing to endure punishment if it meant getting to do what he wanted. However, he also recognized his limits – graduating high school was important to him and he even had hopes of going to college, although that would have seemed like an impossible dream for a young man with no money in those days. As George grew older, he gave more and more thought to what he would do once he graduated high school. Jobs were limited and he wanted more than what the town of Berry had to offer him at the time. George was a nice-looking young man who was particular about his appearance. He often wore his hat a little cocked on his head and a smile on his face. Finding a wife would not have been difficult for him, but he recognized the difficulty of supporting a family and wanted something more than having to work all the time like his father had to do.

With the limited opportunities for George in Berry, Alabama and the surrounding area, joining the navy was probably one of the few good alternatives for him at the time. Joining the navy meant a regular paycheck and job security, but George was also interested in learning a skill or trade, and the Navy Hospital Corpsman School seemed to fit the bill. As a navy corpsman he would receive training as a medical assistant, learning first aid, anatomy, medical care, and hygiene, how to operate medical equipment, and even assist doctors with surgery. Their training revolved around how to keep the wounded in combat areas alive until more professional medical care was available. This often meant putting their own lives in danger. Thousands of lives were saved in WWII as a result of the training and dedication of the corpsmen and medics, many of whom lost their lives while trying to assist others on the battlefield.

Just a week after his 19th birthday, in February 1931, George joined the navy and began basic training at the U.S. Naval Training Station at Portsmouth, Virginia. More than likely, this was the furthest he had ever been from home up to that point. While it had to have been an exciting experience for a young man from the town of Berry, George would also have had to be somewhat apprehensive. Back in Berry, he would have known just about everyone and most of the people there shared a somewhat similar background. Here in his new surroundings, there would have been people from all over the country with various backgrounds and ethnic identities. With the large influx of European immigrants who had been arriving over the prior decades, it was not uncommon to still associate people with their families' national origin, i.e., a German, Pole, Swede, Frenchman, Greek, etc. George might have seemed surprised if his fellow cadets commented on his southern accent since he probably thought that they were the ones with the strange way of using English. Although George tended to be on the quiet side in his new surroundings, he was well liked by his fellow cadets. He was quickly gaining an education, some good and some not so good. If he had ever heard the phrase, "cuss like a sailor", he would have quickly understood what it meant after joining the service. After spending over three months in basic training, George was not only much more physically fit, but had acquired a much broader vocabulary and world view.

After his stint in basic training, George was accepted into the Hospital Corps School in Virginia where he received over five months of medical corpsmen training. Growing up in a small southern town without a lot of opportunity and with the Great Depression in full swing, he appreciated the chance at having a steady job and one that provided training towards a career, as well as one with a noble purpose.

George, being seven and a half years older than Max, had the opportunity for various assignments and additional training before being sent overseas before the start of the war. A summary of his assignments follows:

- U.S. Naval Hospital, Portsmouth, Virginia from 10-30-1931 to 11-15-1936; Ward duties, Master at Arms.
- USS *Wyoming*, from 11-15-1936 to 10-20-1938; Operating Room, Clerical Office, General Duties.
- U.S. Marine Barracks, Quantico, Virginia from 10-30-1938 to 3-15-1939; X-Ray Dept., Field duty with Marines.
- U.S. Naval Hospital, Brooklyn, New York from 3-19-1939 to 6-16-1939; In charge GSK.
- Embalming School, Philadelphia, Pennsylvania from 6-20-1939 to 9-21-1939.
- U.S. Naval Hospital, Portsmouth, Virginia from 9-25-1939 to 10-15-1939; Awaiting transportation to the Asiatic station.
- USS *Henderson* from 10-15-1939 to 1-26-1940; Transportation.
- U.S. Naval Hospital, Canacao, Philippine Islands, from 1-26-1940 to 4-15-1940; MAA OOD's Office. Attended chemical warfare school while stationed at Canacao.
- USS *Tulsa* from 4-16-40 to 11-25-1940; Laboratory, Clerical Office. (At this time the USS *Tulsa* was being used as part of the South China Patrol to observe conditions along the South China

coast following the outbreak of Sino-Japanese war that started in July 1937.)

- U.S. Naval Hospital, Canacao, Philippine Islands from 11-25-1940 to 11-25-1941, Information Desk, Record Office.
- Dispensary, Manila, Philippine Islands from 4-30-1941 to 1-1-1942.

As can be seen from the above list of George's stations, training, and work responsibilities, he was acquiring a broad range of skills. He not only took great pride in doing a job right but seemed to have been eager to learn new skills that would serve him well later in his career.

During George's service on the USS *Wyoming*, it was used for conducting training cruises for midshipmen and NROTC cadets to a number of destinations including European ports, the Panama Canal, and Pacific coast. In 1937, while conducting war exercises off the coast of California a terrible tragedy occurred. A 5-inch shrapnel shell that was being loaded into one of the guns exploded, killing six marines and wounding another 11. This would give George his first real exposure to treating men with severe injuries and a foretaste of what he would experience later during the war.

As noted earlier, George had five sisters and was particularly close to Thelma and Aller. Thelma was a year older than George and Aller was about two years younger. The next sister, Gene, was born about seven years after Aller, and then followed by Willie Nell and Billie Dove. Like their brother, Thelma and Aller chose to put off marriage and focus on careers for themselves. Three of George's sisters, Thelma, Aller, and Gene, would become nurses, and like him, join the military.

For a couple of years after graduating high school, Thelma and Aller helped their parents with taking care of the younger children and the farm but decided that there had to be a better way of making a living. George spoke highly of his role as a medical corpsman, so the sisters became interested in becoming nurses and working in the medical field as well. The only problem was that they had next to no money for nursing school. However, the family did have a good reputation in their small community. With that, and a little courage and self-confidence, the

Brothers Born of Adversity

sisters went to Mr. Cannon who owned one of the mercantile stores in town. They managed to persuade him to grant them a loan to go to nursing school, which they would repay after graduating nursing school and training in Birmingham. Their first nursing jobs were at St. Luke's Hospital in Jacksonville, Florida. A couple of years prior to the start of WWII, Thelma and Aller met a retired army officer and his wife who told them about the advantages of becoming army nurses. This interested the sisters, so they applied, were accepted, and became U.S. Army nurses, beginning their military career at Fort Benning, Georgia.

In March 1941, now army nurses, Thelma and Aller were transferred to Puerto Rico to work. After the start of the war, the military began setting up bases and hospitals in the West Indies, where many of the GI's would be trained before they were sent overseas. As a result, the sisters were transferred to the Caribbean Island of Antigua where they would spend the next couple of years continuing to work as nurses and honing their skills.

Although Max was born and raised less than 60 miles away from the Crowell family, his upbringing was quite different. Max was born in Birmingham, Alabama on August 25, 1919, in their family home. His father, Frank Maxwell, worked for the railroad and his mother, Pernie Lee, was a popular hairdresser. Max was their only child. They lived on the north side of Birmingham in a brick house with large front and back porches and a separate garage in the backyard. In 1929, the Great Depression began, which devastated many lives. Sadly, a couple years into the Depression, Max's father committed suicide by shooting himself. Tragically, 12-year-old Max was the one to find him. Often the children of parents who commit suicide, or other traumatic acts, or even divorce, can take on some of the guilt and shame of what their parent(s) had done. For Max, this may have led him to compensate by feeling the need to be as perfect as possible to prove he was worthy of respect. Of course, he wanted to do all he could to comfort his mother and to make her proud of him as well. Fortunately for Max, he had a loving and nurturing mother who continued to make ends meet as a hairdresser working from their home. Max would also take small jobs to earn money to help his mother out. In high school Max learned shorthand and occasionally earned money as a stenographer.

Brothers Born of Adversity

Living in a larger city during the Depression, Max would remember seeing poor and unemployed people standing in long lines for food. Often hungry people would show up at their back door where his mother would share biscuits and gravy or whatever she had with them. Max's mother had a strong Christian faith and attended a local Baptist church every Sunday morning and Wednesday night. Max grew up with a strong Christian faith as well, although he admitted that at times in his life he had wandered away. But in later life he became a fully committed Christian again. Max had a strong belief that it was his faith in God that got him through his terrible years of imprisonment during the war.

Growing up in an industrial city which was producing coal, iron, and steel, it was not uncommon to have soot and ash raining down on various parts of the city from the mills, depending on the direction of the wind. As a tribute to the area's iron and steel industry, a 56-foot-tall cast iron statue depicting Vulcan, the Roman god of fire and the forging of metal, was commissioned. While initially the statue was exhibited in the 1904 World's Fair in St. Louis, Missouri, it was eventually taken back to Birmingham, where it would be reassembled and stand at the fairgrounds until the late 1920's, when it was disassembled for inspection. Lying unassembled for several years, it was a favorite place of play and exploration for children like Max at the time. In the late 1930's the statue was given a permanent home in a park on Red Mountain, overlooking the city of Birmingham on a 126-foot pedestal.

Max joined the Alabama National Guard while still in high school, at the age of 16. After graduating high school and exploring career paths, Max decided he wanted to join the navy and become a navy corpsman. The caring and nurturing qualities Max had developed growing up seemed to make him a perfect fit for such a role. Experiencing the tragic loss of his father at a young age, probably, to some extent, gave him the fortitude to deal with the horrors of war he would experience later.

Max enlisted in the navy on March 23, 1938, and underwent recruit training for the next three months at Norfolk, Virginia. From July 1938 to the end of October 1938, he attended hospital corpsmen instruction at the U.S. Navy Hospital Corps School in San Diego, California. From there he was assigned to the U.S. Navy Hospital at Pensacola, Florida until June 30, 1939, doing general duties of a hospital apprentice and clerical work. Next, he was transferred to San Francisco, California where he would be assigned to the USS *Chaumont* for transport to the Philippines, making stops in Honolulu and Guam before arriving in Manila on August 16, 1939.

In order to become navy corpsmen, it would have been necessary for George and Max to take the Corpsman's Pledge. They would not have taken this pledge lightly and it would have continued to influence their behavior and actions even while prisoners of war. The pledge that they took follows:

> ### *Corpsman's Pledge*
> *"I solemnly pledge myself before God and these witnesses to practice faithfully all of my duties as a member of the Hospital Corps. I hold the care of the sick and injured to be a privilege and a sacred trust and will assist the Medical Officer with loyalty and honesty. I will not knowingly permit harm to come to any patient. I will not partake of nor administer any unauthorized medication. I will hold all personal matters pertaining to the private lives of patients in strict confidence. I dedicate my heart, mind, and strength to the work before me. I shall do all within my power to show in myself an example of all that is honorable and good throughout my naval career."*

By 1939, the United States military presence was being expanded in the Pacific as tensions were increasing with the Empire of Japan. As a result of this expansion, both George and Max would be given overseas assignments to the same navy base near Manila, the capital of the Philippines. Since Max was already in California, he was shipped out several months ahead of George. By late 1939 George was stationed in San Francisco, preparing for transport to the Philippines with stops in Hawaii and China before reaching his destination. Using stationery from the army and navy branch of Young Men's Christian Association in San Francisco, George mailed a letter back home to his mother on November 23, 1939, which read as follows:

Brothers Born of Adversity

"Dear Home:
Wondering why I have not heard from you all lately. I am
well and doing fair, on my way to the far east. We leave
Frisco, Calif. on the 3rd of December. My address will be
as follows ….
  George Crowell Phm.2/c
  USS Henderson
  Of. Post Master
  San Francisco, California.

While we are here in Calif. it will take 3 or 4 days to hear
from you by air mail 6 cent stamps. After we reach China
it will take about 1 mo. to rec. mail from you. Air mail will
cost around 50 or 60 cents. It will come by the China
Clipper quicker.

How's every one making out these days. Hope all is
enjoying good health. Dad still on the water wagon –
really hope he stays on it. Grandpah still dickering
around, hope he is still on top of the earth when I return…

Hoping to hear from you people real soon. Give all I
know my best. Regards. Love You All, Wyman"

Then, the day before he was to leave, George wrote a much more affectionate letter to his parents and placed it in the clothes that he was sending back home to them. It read in part as follows:

"To the Sweetest and Best Mother in all the World. As you
look through my pocket of this coat Dear Mother and Dad
remember that your only son, even if he is a million miles
away always thinks of you both. Give all the Sis's a big
kiss and hug for me.
Oceans of Love, Wyman Crowell"

It was an emotional time for George. This was to be a longer overseas assignment than what he had experienced in the past, and there were rumors of a possible war, and he had to wonder when and if he would ever see his family again. As he was waiting there in San Francisco and preparing for his departure it struck him just how much he loved his family. Expressing his feelings wasn't easy for George, but he didn't want to miss the chance to tell his parents how much he loved them in case he was never to see them again. Perhaps hiding this more affectionate letter in the clothes he was sending back home made it easier for him to send.

After Max's arrival in the Philippines, and some months later George's arrival, they were assigned to the Canacao Naval Hospital. The hospital was near the naval yard or base at Cavite City, a peninsula extending out into Manila Bay on the south end of the city of Manila. It was probably during this time that George and Max met.

The grounds at Canacao Navy Hospital consisted of 36 acres along the bay. The grounds were beautiful, with stately shade trees, flowering shrubs, and colorful plants. Running along the sea wall of the bay were lamps resembling Japanese stone temple lanterns, which provided light at night. Being located along the bay, the navy hospital had the advantage of a consistent cool breeze, in an otherwise hot and humid climate. Many senior military officers at the time would request to be assigned there a few years prior to retirement as a way of winding down their military career while enjoying the climate and Filipino culture. This would later prove to be a big mistake, not just for these officers, but for the military as a whole. For newcomers like George and Max, the place seemed like a paradise and a good assignment. The Filipino people were pleasant and likeable. George had even met a young Filipino woman who he was seeing, and all seemed good at the time. However, everything was to change dramatically after the Japanese declared war on the United States.

While stationed at Canacao Naval Hospital, George left for a seven-month stint on the USS *Tulsa*, which was part of the South China Patrol monitoring the South China coastline. Once back at the Canacao Hospital, George would be assigned to work at the nearby dispensary at the navy yard up until the time of the Japanese invasion. Likewise, Max had spent some months before the start of the war assigned to the cruiser USS

Brothers Born of Adversity

Houston, until December 1, 1941. Once he had returned to Manila, he was assigned to the USS *Napa AT-32,* a seagoing tug.

Within a week of Max's return to Manila from his duty on the USS *Houston,* the war in the Pacific began. Less than three months later the USS *Houston* would be sunk by the Japanese with only 368 members of a crew of 1,061 surviving. The surviving members were all captured by the Japanese and, of those, 77 died in captivity. Max more than likely would have learned the fate of the USS *Houston* and thought himself lucky that he had been transferred off that ship, not aware that he would later survive two ship sinkings and some of the most brutal treatment imaginable.

The photo below shows part of the Canacao Hospital and Navy Station, where George and Max were assigned prior to the war. The photo was sent to George's family by Ernest Irvin, a fellow POW and hell ship survivor. It is probably an old military photograph of the area. On the back he states, *"This aerial photo was taken sometime in 1937 – please note 3 low frequency radio towers used to communicate with our submarines till 12/16/41 when one tower was knocked down and hospital damaged by Japanese bombers."*

Chapter 2 - Prelude to War

To better understand the nature of the war with Japan it is useful to have a basic understanding of events leading up to WWII. Beginning in the mid-19th century as Japan began interacting with western powers, they started adopting many western political, judicial, military, and cultural ideas. Japan expanded economically with the adoption of a market economy and became the most developed nation in Asia. After success in the First Sino-Japanese War (1894-1895) and the Russo-Japanese War (1904-1905), Japan controlled Formosa (Taiwan), Korea, and part of Sakhalin Island, which had been part of Russia. Japan joined the Allies in World War I, capturing German possessions, and made advances into China.

As the early 20th century began, Japan had become very militaristic and more hostile toward the ideas of democracy. Although Japan was ruled by a monarch who was considered quasi-divine, military and business interests had considerable influence on the emperor and the government. Michinomiya Hirohito, who became emperor in 1926 and ruled until 1989, was worshiped as a god by the Japanese people. Some argue that Hirohito was not interested in running the affairs of state and took a hands-off approach, allowing his ministers, particularly the military, to run the government. Others would disagree with this and would say he was more involved in planning the war than what he wanted to admit. In any event, the leadership wanted Japan to be a powerful nation and, although they had a population of 70 million people by 1935, they lacked many of the natural resources needed to fulfill their ambition.

In 1931, Japan invaded Manchuria, the northern part of what is known as China today and, after receiving international condemnation for it, withdrew from the League of Nations in 1933. Also, significant to note is that Japan never ratified the 1929 Geneva Convention, an international agreement on how prisoners of war were to be treated. After WWII started, Japan announced that they would adhere to the Geneva Convention but, in reality, they seemed to feel no obligation to treat prisoners of war in the manner prescribed by the agreement. This contributed to the horrendous treatment that George, Max, and the other POWs experienced at the hands of their Japanese captors. In one

Brothers Born of Adversity

comparison examined, the death rate of POWs held by the Germans during WWII was said to be 1.2 percent, while in the Pacific Theater of war with the Japanese the rate was said to be 37 percent, and even slightly higher for those imprisoned in the Philippines.

By 1936 Japan had started aligning with Germany and the Axis Powers, and the rift with the Allied powers grew worse. In 1937, Japan invaded other parts of China initiating the Second Sino-Japanese War (1937-1945). The Japanese military was ruthless in its conquests, killing millions, resulting in some labeling it the "Asian Holocaust." Numerous instances of large-scale massacres by the Japanese military were reported. The most well-known of these relates to the capture of the Chinese capital Nanjing. There the Japanese troops committed terrible atrocities, including the rape and the brutal massacre of about a quarter million citizens. It is believed that these atrocities were sanctioned by the military leadership. This would later become known as the "Rape of Nanjing." The Japanese waged vast amounts of devastation on the Chinese people and even used biological warfare against them - spreading diseases such as cholera, typhoid, dysentery, and the plague; as well as using chemical weapons against them.

There were numerous reports of women being taken from captive regions and used by the military troops as "comfort women" or sex slaves. Special units of the Japanese military were known to have conducted inhumane experiments on civilians and POWs, including removing limbs without anesthesia and the testing of biological weapons. The Japanese military was tough, disciplined, and fanatical in the way they waged war. The Japanese were taught to believe that their emperor was divine and that they were destined to rule the world. They would try to justify their expansion activities as being little different than the colonization done by western powers.

At this time, many countries, including the United States, had a significant civilian population, as well as military personnel, stationed in Shanghai, China. Shanghai was an important international trading center on the Chinese coast, only about 200 miles east of Nanjing. George probably spent some time in Shanghai before being sent on to the Philippines. Recognizing the growing tensions with Japan, many

Brothers Born of Adversity

American civilians working in Shanghai sent their families back to the States, and as tensions escalated further, American workers returned to the States as well.

In 1940 Japan invaded French Indochina, which was made up of what is now Vietnam, Cambodia, and Laos. In response, the United States placed an oil embargo on Japan and froze Japanese assets. At the time, Japan was dependent upon the United States for its oil supplies and now needed their captured lands in Southeast Asia even more to provide it with oil. The Japanese responded by sending negotiators to Washington under the pretense of wanting to negotiate, while instead initiating plans for the attack on Pearl Harbor and other targets in the Pacific.

In 1941 the United States Pacific Fleet was stationed at Pearl Harbor on the Hawaiian Island of Oahu, just west of Honolulu. The harbor at times could have over 90 U.S. warships and several hundred aircraft stationed at three airfields nearby. Prior to the war, being stationed in Hawaii would have been considered a great assignment and would have been a stop for George and Max before heading to the Philippines. The U.S. military had a false sense of security in thinking that Hawaii would be an unlikely target since the Japanese planes could not fly there, let alone return, from any of their existing airbases. Eight or nine years prior to the attack on Pearl Harbor, the U.S. military conducted a feasibility test by launching planes off aircraft carriers in a mock surprise attack on Pearl Harbor. Had it been an actual attack the Pacific Fleet would have been wiped out, but apparently nobody paid any attention to the drill -- except maybe the Japanese.

Another important U.S. military presence in the Pacific was in the Philippine Islands. The Philippines consists of 7,000 islands with the majority of the population on the 11 largest islands. The islands' population spoke 175 different languages which made communication and coordination more difficult once the war started. Luzon is the largest of the islands and the most populated. It is also the most northern of the islands and is the location of Manila, the capital city of the Philippines, which lies along Manila Bay with its deep-water port. The area terrain is varied with mountains, plains, and coral reefs. Manila is 5,000 miles from Pearl Harbor in Hawaii, but only 1,800 miles from Tokyo, the capital of

Brothers Born of Adversity

Japan. In the early 1900s the Army Corps of Engineers created land along Manila Bay from low-tide mud flats and built Pier 7 which became a significant landmark along the bay known as the "Million Dollar Pier." Across the bay and to the west of Manila lay the Bataan Peninsula and the Island of Corregidor off its coast.

Postcard showing Pier 7 before the war, known as the "Million Dollar Pier." Public domain photo.

The Philippines had been occupied by American military forces since 1898 with the defeat of Spanish forces in the Philippines during the Spanish American War. In 1935 the Islands were granted commonwealth status and Manuel Quezon was elected as their first President. Full independence was scheduled for 1946. With commonwealth status the Philippines began the establishment of their own defense forces. Decorated WWI war hero, and former Army Chief of Staff, General Douglas MacArthur had come out of retirement in 1937 to help the commonwealth organize their defense forces and oversee American military forces on the Islands. MacArthur believed that the Philippines were of critical strategic importance to the United States. Frustrated with lack of funding and support for his efforts in the Philippines, he again went into retirement only to be called back to duty by President Roosevelt in mid-1941 as concerns of Japanese aggression increased.

26

Brothers Born of Adversity

The Philippine Islands are on the other side of the international date line, so as the sun broke on the Eastern horizon at Pearl Harbor on December 7, 1941, it was already December 8th in Manila.

Brothers Born of Adversity

Chapter 3 - The U.S. Enters the War & George and Max's Imprisonment Begins

December 7, 1941, began as a beautiful Sunday morning in Hawaii, a U.S. territory at the time. Many of the residents at the Pearl Harbor naval base were moving at a leisurely pace, preparing for church, or sleeping in. Meanwhile, the Japanese 6th fleet was beginning their planned two-wave attack with over 350 planes being launched from aircraft carriers about 200 miles north of the island. As the Japanese began their first wave of attack there were over 90 American warships of various kinds at anchorage in the bay at Pearl Harbor. The Japanese attack caught the United States by surprise, and the resulting damage to the American fleet was immense. American aircraft took an equal beating as most were simply parked on the ground when the invasion started. Over 2,400 Americans were killed, missing, or mortally wounded, while an additional 1,200 were less seriously wounded. On this day, the United States had suffered a terrible defeat. Fortunately, the U.S. aircraft carriers were away at the time of the attack and important base installations had not been destroyed by the Japanese. As part of the Japanese coordinated effort, attacks also began on the Philippines, Guam, and Wake Island, as well as the British Empire in Malaya, Singapore, and Hong Kong. Later that same day, Japan announced a declaration of war on the United States, but the declaration was not delivered until the following day. On December 8, 1941, President Franklin Roosevelt gave his famous "Day of Infamy" speech, which was broadcast to the nation, and war was declared against the Empire of Japan.

The area in WWII where the Allies fought the Japanese Empire is often referred to as the Pacific Theater and extended from Northern China and the Aleutian Islands of Alaska in the north to India in the west, most of the island nations of the Pacific and Indian Oceans, and as far south as Australia. It was the largest theater of war during WWII. Japan's conquest of China had begun years earlier resulting in the Chinese Nationalist Party and Chinese Communist Party putting their civil war temporarily on hold to fight the Japanese.

28

Brothers Born of Adversity

After General MacArthur's return to the Philippines in mid-1941, he started preparations for the possibility of a war with Japan and a potential invasion of the Philippines, but preparations were far from complete by the time the war broke out. Prior to the war, military strategists had developed plans to follow in the event of a war with Japan. The plans provided for American and Filipino forces to retreat into the fortifications on Corregidor and Bataan. Both locations were to be well stocked with enough food, necessary supplies, and ammunition to withstand a siege of six months or longer. As General MacArthur began preparation for the defense of the Philippines, he thought that the plans that had been laid out were defeatist and that he could protect a large portion of the Philippines by dividing his troops and placing them strategically around the Islands. However, soon after the fighting began, he realized that was a mistake. Anticipating that the Japanese might try to destroy their bombers and fighter planes by sabotage, many of them had been grouped close together where they would be easier to guard. Unfortunately, this made them much easier targets for the Japanese bombers. Additionally, many of the planes had just recently arrived in crates and hadn't been assembled by the time of the invasion. Some American pilots were able to get their planes in the air, but they were outnumbered and no match for overwhelming Japanese invasion forces.

As word of the bombing of Pearl Harbor reached MacArthur and staff, it became quite apparent that the Philippines would be next. Within hours of the attack on Pearl Harbor, attacks began on some of the outlying bases on the Philippine Islands. The Canacao Navy Hospital in the Manila area was near the navy yard, which the military command realized would soon become a target. Immediate arrangements were made to start moving the patients from the navy hospital to a less desirable target for the Japanese. Ambulatory patients were called back to duty and the other patients were sent to Sternberg Army Hospital in downtown Manila. Anticipating a possible threat, military dependents had been sent State-side a few months earlier. This resulted in the dependent's ward of the hospital being available for those being transferred from Canacao. Although assigned to the Canacao Hospital, George had been serving at the dispensary at the naval yard for the past eight months. Now the dispensary was being prepared as a battle dressing station for the navy yard area, recognizing that it would be a primary target when the

Brothers Born of Adversity

Japanese began attacks on the Manila area. Meanwhile, while George was serving at the dispensary, Max had been assigned to a naval vessel named the USS *Napa AT-32*, working off the coast of the Bataan Peninsula and Corregidor.

On the morning of December 10th, the bombing of the navy yard began. The high-flying Japanese bombers, which were out of the range of American gunners below, seemed unstoppable as they bombed the navy yard and other targets in the area. One veteran recalled seeing the incoming planes and commenting about their beautiful formation, not initially recognizing that they were Japanese airplanes until the bombs started dropping. George along with other military staff quickly took shelter in underground bunkers until the first wave of bombing was over. Much of the navy yard had been blown into the bay, lay in rubble, or had gone up in flames. The bombing and strafing also resulted in over 1,000 dead and wounded. George felt lucky to have survived the attack, but now he and other available corpsmen needed to focus on treating the injured and getting them transferred back to Canacao Navy Hospital; it had surprisingly not been touched during the first wave of attacks. Realizing they would probably not be so lucky during the next attack, military command directed that the wounded be moved to the Sternberg Army hospital located in Manila along the Pasig River.

The bombings and strafing would continue in waves. In between raids by the Japanese bombers and fighters, George and his fellow corpsmen would search for wounded and scavenge the Canacao Hospital for medical and other supplies that would be needed at Sternberg Army Hospital. Many of George's fellow corpsmen were killed or wounded during their efforts to treat and rescue the wounded on the base and in the surrounding area. For most of the corpsmen it was their first experience serving in combat conditions and treating the kind of injuries they were now having to deal with. Since George had been in the service longer than most of the other corpsmen and had actual experience in dealing with such severely injured individuals, he would have certainly played a leadership role in tending to the wounded. The Sternberg Army Hospital was soon overflowing with the injured, so several other buildings nearby were taken over for hospital use. Crews were set up to bury the dead, which were quick to swell and decompose in the tropical heat.

Brothers Born of Adversity

Some bodies had been blown to pieces. One lieutenant involved in processing the dead gave each of his men whiskey as fortification in doing such an unpleasant task. A local Jai Alai pavilion was set up as a morgue. Doctors and corpsmen worked countless hours in an effort to treat as many patients as possible.

By December 24th, realizing he could not defend a broad area of the Philippine Islands, General MacArthur had started moving his forces to the Bataan peninsula and the island fortress of Corregidor. (See the map on the following page.) This resulted in vast amounts of military personnel and supplies needing to be moved through Manila to be transported out to Bataan and Corregidor. As a result, it was necessary that George and those assigned to the dispensary at the navy yard maintain their position. This was necessary to provide medical assistance to those injured from the continued bombings and strafing as military units continued moving through the city and to the docks. By December 27th, it was necessary to move the dispensary to the Manila Yacht Club along Manila Bay as a result of the continued bombings at the navy yard.

Brothers Born of Adversity

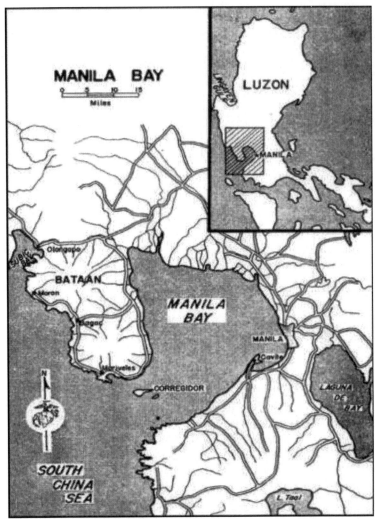

Map of Manila Bay area showing the locations of the city of Manila, Cavite, Bataan, and Corregidor. Public domain map.

To minimize the destruction of Manila and its population, the city was declared an "Open City" as defined by the Hague Convention of 1907, an international agreement on the conduct of war. This meant that American and Philippine troops would be removed from the city and that the Japanese would be free to occupy it without any resistance and that any remaining American military personnel in the city would surrender. While it might have brought some comfort in believing that this would stop the air raids on the city, it also meant that George and the other medical staff left behind to care for the patients at the Sternberg Army Hospital would soon become prisoners of the Japanese Empire.

Picture showing "Open City" sign above a street in Manila.
Public domain photo.

Despite the city of Manila being declared an open city, the Japanese continued to bomb targets along the Pasig River, which runs through the city.

The Sternberg Army Hospital was an old wooden structure that had been built along the banks of the river. On December 28, 1941, fearing that the hospital might get bombed, the chief medical command decided to move the remaining patients and staff from the hospital to Santa Escolastica and other nearby facilities further from the river. Santa Escolastica had been a Catholic women's college prior to this time. On

Brothers Born of Adversity

December 29th George and the rest of the dispensary personnel at the Manila Yacht Club were also directed to move to Santa Escolastica before the Japanese arrived.

Prior to the surrender of the city, the remaining hospital staff were given a choice to be transferred to the Bataan Peninsula or Corregidor or remain in the hospital in Manila with the realization that they would soon become prisoners of the Japanese Empire. Many of the highest-ranking medical officers chose to remain with their patients in Manila. Although they would become prisoners of the Japanese sooner, it also meant they would not be involved in the heavy fighting that they knew would be occurring on Bataan and Corregidor. To minimize the chances of altercations when the Japanese arrived, the medical officers went through the wards instructing patients and corpsmen alike on how they were to act when the Japanese arrived. All guns, knives, and other weapons were collected and placed in a pile to minimize the chances of someone doing something regrettable. This was also done to show the Japanese their intentions of not attempting any resistance.

Early on the morning of January 3, 1942, a Japanese soldier began pounding on the entry gate to the Santa Escolastica but did not enter or say anything to the staff. The medical staff had placed red crosses and white flags on all sides of the building. Later in the day as Japanese troops assembled out in front of the compound, an American doctor serving as commanding officer went out of the compound with his hands held high to meet the Japanese troops. Japanese soldiers then entered the hospital compound with bayonets affixed to their rifles. Once inside they searched the wards taking medical supplies and other personal items, as well as the stash of weapons that had been placed in a pile. Since it was still January 2, 1942, in Hawaii, George and his fellow prisoners marked January 2, as the start of their imprisonment by the Japanese Empire, less than a month from when the United States entered the war.

The Japanese placed guards at the Santa Escolastica compound, which now functioned as a military prison camp, as well as hospital for the POWs. Routine inspections were carried out by the Japanese of their prisoners, during which time they continued to confiscate items they wanted. Some semblance of military life was allowed to continue, although the Americans were required to stay in the compound and not to be anywhere near the outside walls where the Japanese were now stationed. On March 23, 1942, without much notice, George and some of his fellow prisoners were marched about a mile away to Pasay Elementary School, which would serve as their new temporary prison. Others followed over the next couple of weeks. It seemed the Japanese thought Santa Escolastica was too good for their American prisoners. The Pasay school was filthy and inadequate for the number of prisoners who started arriving there.

In 1945, after the Allied Forces had liberated the Philippines, several military records were found on Corregidor, including a typed page by George, titled "Bilibid Prison". It reads as follows:

"The suddenness of the war's coming naturally shocked me and knocked me off balance for a short space of time. But one can become used to anything. In due time, I normally, with the usual interest, continued to carry out my various duties as has been my habit throughout my navy career.

Due to the situation, I have managed to keep very busy and have not allowed myself to dwell too often on thoughts of home. And of my former life. I consider the temporary loss of these as a sacrifice that must be made towards an end, and I am sure that one day I will be repaid. The coming of Red Cross supplies and mail from home have helped tremendously to give life to the dull monotonous routine I have endured. I know they haven't forgotten and are patiently waiting for our return."

It's not entirely clear when or why George would have written the statement. Possibly it was a staff exercise to evaluate how the men were handling the stress of the war and the situation they were in. In any event, it does provide insight into how George attempted to deal with the stress and monotony.

While George and his fellow prisoners in Manila were trying to adjust to life as POWs, the fighting remained fierce on the Bataan Peninsula and island fortress of Corregidor for several more months. The Bataan

Brothers Born of Adversity

Peninsula is approximately 25 miles long and 20 miles wide at its widest point and juts out into the west side of Manila Bay and is directly across the bay from the city of Manila. The terrain is mountainous with jungles, gullies, and streams running across it. On the south end of Bataan is a smaller bay named Mariveles Bay, which was heavily used and protected by the Allied forces until Bataan fell.

Across the entrance to Manila Bay, the United States military had established four island fortresses. The largest of these island fortresses was Corregidor, officially named Fort Mills, which was situated about two miles off the Bataan coast. Corregidor was a tadpole-shaped island about 3.5 miles long and 1.5 miles wide across at its widest section, with an elevation of 589 feet at its highest point. Hundreds of feet of tunnel works had been built into Malinta Hill, the high point on the island, including room for a 1,000-bed underground hospital. Additionally, the island fortress was equipped with an extensive arsenal of weapons organized into 23 batteries. Generally, when speaking of Corregidor, it is in reference to all four of the island fortifications. Beginning December 29, 1941, the aerial bombardment of Corregidor began, which destroyed many of the barracks, the above ground hospital, and other facilities on the island. Food and water rations would increasingly become scarcer for the defenders. When horses belonging to the cavalry were killed in the bombardments their carcasses would be dragged to the mess hall for consumption.

It is interesting to note that the island fortress of Corregidor held 20 tons of gold and silver, as well as securities and other important documents which had been removed from Philippine banks to keep the Japanese from seizing it. In February 1942, the United States was able to deliver 3,500 rounds of ammunition to Corregidor on the submarine, USS *Trout*, and remove the gold and silver and other valuables from the island. After loading her cargo, the USS *Trout* submerged to the bottom of Manila Bay until dark and then was escorted out to open water by defending naval vessels.

The next largest island fortress was Fort Hughes on Caballo Island, which lay just south of Corregidor. Although the island only consisted of about 160 acres it rose out of the bay to a height of 380 feet. The two remaining island fortresses were Fort Drum on El Fraile Island and Fort Frank on Carabao Island. Each of these island fortifications had been well fortified and equipped with defensive weapons. The military had long considered Bataan and these island fortifications great defensive locations. However, in the hasty plans to take advantage of the location they were not properly supplied with food, ammunition, medical supplies, and other necessary equipment for a long siege. At the beginning of 1942, Bataan and the island fortifications held 80,000 Allied troops and 26,000 civilians with only about a 30-day supply of food.

The battle for Bataan and Corregidor was vicious, and the heroic defenders held their ground into March, even though they were weak and nearly starved from lack of adequate food. Recognizing that the Philippines would soon be lost to the Japanese, President Roosevelt ordered General MacArthur to leave Corregidor for Australia. Using PT boats, General MacArthur, his family, and staff, made their escape. Although reluctant to leave, he followed President Roosevelt's orders but swore to those left behind that he would return. On April 9, 1942, realizing that prolonging the fight would simply increase the casualty rate, General King, who commanded the troops on Bataan, surrendered. On May 6, 1942, General Wainwright, who was responsible for the troops on Corregidor, also surrendered.

For the first couple of weeks after joining the undermanned American and Filipino crew on the USS *Napa AT-32,* Max assisted with laying down and maintaining mine and anti-torpedo netting across the entrance to Mariveles Bay on the coast of Bataan, and also in Manila Bay. Additionally, the Napa crew ran fuel to ships around Manila Bay until the fuel ran out. Often, they were under heavy enemy fire. Although the Napa was undermanned, the crew inexperienced, and the work dangerous, they were successful in accomplishing most of the net laying they were charged with before they were told to cease operations. Over the next couple of months, the Napa crew operated out of Mariveles on the Bataan coast; performing patrols, towing, salvage, and net maintenance. The gun deck of the Napa had been refitted with a 50-caliber machine gun mounted between two three-inch guns and would be involved in direct enemy combat, having 10 confirmed kills and four more probable kills, without incurring any casualties among its crew.

Brothers Born of Adversity

Despite near misses from enemy gunfire and bombings, Max and the rest of the Napa crew continued their operations out of Mariveles until just before Bataan fell on April 9, 1942. The day before Bataan fell the crew was ordered to sink the Napa off the coast of Corregidor and using smaller boats evacuated the crew and provisions to Corregidor where they were incorporated into the 4th Marine Regiment in manning the beach defenses. Upon the surrender of Bataan, the Japanese assembled the prisoners captured from Bataan, whether sick, wounded, or dying, at the Mariveles harbor area. They then set up their heavy artillery behind the captured troops and began firing at Corregidor from that location. Learning of this cruel and illegal act, the defenders of Corregidor did not fire back until the POWs were removed and had begun their infamous Bataan Death March. It has been said that Corregidor was one of the most intensely bombed places in the history of warfare.

On April 10, 1942, while Corregidor was being heavily shelled, Max and a number of other men were transported to Ft. Hughes on the little island of Caballo, in sight of Corregidor. There, Max and the other men scuttled their vessels and joined the men under the command of Commander Bridget who was in charge of the beach defenses. Max was assigned to help operate the mortars and big guns, which they used to fire at enemy targets. Like Corregidor, Ft. Hughes was routinely bombed and strafed by Japanese planes. Max and the other forces at Caballo watched the constant bombardment of Corregidor and wondered how much longer it could hold out. The big fear was a night invasion when it would be hard to see the enemy landing on the beach. On Corregidor, a powerful search light would be turned on for 10 to 15 seconds to scan the Bataan coast for invasion forces but would then be quickly turned off and retracted into a concrete cave, since the light would draw immediate fire from the Japanese.

On May 5, 1942, the invasion of Corregidor began with intense shelling of the beaches on the north side of the island, which was then followed with the landing of Japanese troops. Unfortunately for the Japanese, they had difficulty with the landings as a result of sea currents and met fierce resistance by the American and Filipino defenders. For the initial invaders it became a blood bath, however their superior forces were eventually able to push the defenders back. Later that day the Japanese landed three armored tanks on the island which were quickly put into action. After fierce and bloody resistance, General Wainwright recognized that to try to hold out one more day would result in the death of thousands of lives, including about 1,000 wounded men inside the Malinta tunnel. Therefore, at about 1:30 p.m. on May 6, 1942, he agreed to surrender his forces on Corregidor and the other three island fortresses. While the battles for Bataan and Corregidor were eventually won by the Japanese, their timetable for the defeat of Australia and the rest of the Pacific had been severely undone by the efforts of the brave defenders of Bataan and Corregidor. The Japanese General Homma, who oversaw the Philippine invasion, was relieved of his command for failing to meet the timetable he had been given.

As word of General Wainwright's surrender reached Commander Bridget at Fort Hughes, steps were immediately taken to destroy as many of the big guns and other equipment as possible and prepare the men as they faced the realization that they would soon become prisoners of the Japanese Empire. Despite the apprehension of surrendering to the Japanese, Max would later recall that initially he didn't think being a prisoner of war was going to be that bad. *"The Jap soldiers were veterans of the China war and they treated us all right. They forced us to adhere to strict regulations and took our jewelry, but they gave free run of the island and we had plenty to eat."* The plentiful food Max referred to was that stored on the island by American military forces in anticipation of the Japanese invasion. Much of it had been buried under the sand to protect it from the attack, as well as to keep it hidden from the Japanese. After the surrender of Fort Hughes, Max was held as a POW on Corregidor and Fort Hughes on Caballo, performing various assignments including general nursing care of American and Japanese patients, serving as a first aid man, and as a laborer for his Japanese captors.

At the end of May and first part of June 1942, George and the other prisoners at Pasay School were moved again, this time to Bilibid Prison in Manila, where they were being joined by many of the men who had surrendered on Bataan and Corregidor. Bilibid had originally been built as a prison by the Spanish in the mid-1800s and prior to WWII was used to store military records. Once the war broke out, Japanese civilians who were living in the Philippines at the time were interned there until the Japanese arrived. The prison had been constructed in the form of a large square compound with 600-foot sides and high perimeter walls with high voltage wires running along the top. Inside the prison the wards and hospital facilities were designed like spokes of a bicycle wheel and divided by a wall through the center of the compound. Upon arrival at Bilibid, George and his fellow captives found themselves among 12,000 weak and sick prisoners in a facility designed for no more than 4,000.

The west half of the prison was used to house the POWs and the east half to house the Japanese military police. Some of the facility had been damaged from bombing and the damaged roofs leaked badly during the heavy rains that occur in the Philippines. Portions of the electrical and plumbing had been stripped from the buildings. A shallow ditch had been dug in an open area to be used as a latrine to accommodate the large number of POWs. Some of the POWs would light heartedly refer to this latrine area as "MacArthur Park." It was often overflowing and full of maggots and flies.

When George first entered Bilibid, the facility was filthy and the stench terrible. POWs already housed there were lying on bare floors covered with flies. Some were sick and others dying. After the Philippines were liberated, a diary that had belonged to a Lt. David Nash, was found near one of the camps. An entry Lt. Nash made on May 25, 1942, while being held in Bilibid read *"We are fortunate enough to be inside although crowded. We sleep on the concrete deck in 4 long lines…. Some men are still living outside in the open but they are the first ones being moved (1,500 at a time)."* Lt. Nash did not survive the war.

George and his fellow corpsmen were soon assigned the task of cleaning the patients, washing the floors, and improving the sanitary conditions at Bilibid. Although the hospital portion of the prison did contain some equipment for needed surgery, medical supplies were in short supply. Quinine, which was used in the treatment of malaria, was in the biggest demand. The Japanese captors posted rules in English for the prisoners to follow and made it clear that violations would be harshly dealt with. Over time a number of repairs and improvements were made at Bilibid, including adding more beds and bedding and improvements in the water system and showers. The following year the Japanese provided insecticides, which were desperately needed to control the bug problem at Bilibid.

The Japanese had established several POW camps throughout the Philippine Islands in order to use POWs as laborers where needed, but Bilibid would serve as the primary hospital facility and clearinghouse for the POWs. As a result, most POWs entering Bilibid would be moved to other camps within a few days after their arrival. The medical department at Bilibid was known as the "U.S. Naval Hospital Unit of Bilibid Prison" and organized as nearly as possible to that of a naval hospital, although under the supervision of the Japanese. The POWs working in the hospital prepared reports required by the Japanese, while also secretly maintaining patient data and personnel records of officers and staff assigned to the hospital. These records were hidden in a crypt behind the reservoir of a toilet built into the prison hospital office. Many of these records were salvaged after the liberation of the Philippines.

George would be among those physicians and medical corpsmen who would be permanently assigned to Bilibid for the next two and a half years to support the hospital operations and administration. As POWs arrived at Bilibid they were searched and most of their personal items were taken from them. They were allowed one uniform, a so called "shelter half", a blanket, as well as mess gear and a spoon that they might have. If they had no mess gear, they had to do with whatever they could find, such as cans, coconut shells, or pieces of metal.

Brothers Born of Adversity

Entrance to Old Bilibid Prison. Public domain photo provided courtesy of National American Defenders of Bataan and Corregidor Museum and Research Center.

Aerial view photo of Old Bilibid Prison. Public domain photo.

Brothers Born of Adversity

While in Bilibid, George and the rest of the medical staff started getting more details on what had happened at Pearl Harbor and were starting to piece together, to some extent, what was going on in the overall war effort. However, if caught discussing such matters in front of their Japanese captors they could expect severe punishment. In addition to the accurate information that they would learn, there would be false information and rumors being circulated as well. A couple of creative former ham radio operators were able to pilfer parts from the Japanese to build a short-wave radio which was a big help in getting news on the war. If caught, it probably would have meant death for those involved. The radio was cleverly hidden under the seat of a stool so as not to be found by the guards. With the help of the radio, the POWs learned about the success of Doolittle's raid in dropping bombs on the Japanese mainland and the American defeat of the Japanese naval forces at Midway Island.

From stories told by survivors of the fighting and surrender of Bataan who started entering Bilibid, George learned just how cruel the Japanese could be. When the American and Filipino military surrendered Bataan, the Japanese quickly realized that they were totally unprepared for the large number of soldiers surrendering. They did not have sufficient food and other supplies necessary for their proper care of so many prisoners. To make matters worse, Japanese culture considered surrender to be a disgrace for any soldier. To them the Bushido Code or "the way of the warrior" meant it was better for a soldier to die fighting than to ever surrender. Some of the Japanese officers thought that all the prisoners should be executed and in many instances their wishes were carried out. The brutal events surrounding the surrender of the American and Filipino soldiers and their forced march of over 60 miles has been referred to as the Bataan Death March and has been the subject of many books and movies. George and the rest of the prisoners being held at Bilibid had to wonder what fate might be awaiting them as well.

While treating patients in Bilibid, medical staff were quickly getting firsthand lessons on treating injuries, as well as many diseases, most of which were related to poor nutrition. Unfortunately, with lack of proper medical supplies they were often limited in what they could do for those who were suffering. The few medical supplies that they did have were strictly rationed for use by those in the most need. The medical staff themselves were not immune to these health issues. While imprisoned at Bilibid, George would contract dengue fever which is transmitted by mosquitos, suffer from beriberi as a result of his poor diet, and suffer from optic neuritis. Additionally, George had an emergency appendectomy while in Bilibid.

Simply having a better diet would have corrected many of the health problems the POWs faced. The diet of the prisoners generally consisted of a cup of rice for breakfast and another cup of rice and a cup of soup for lunch and dinner. The rice was often moldy, contained rocks, stunk, and the soup was no better. Occasionally, they might get some greens or spoiled fish thrown into the mix. However, as the war progressed the rations got even more meager. Some have suggested that despite the hardships at Bilibid they were probably better off overall than many in the other camps. Since Bilibid was the primary hospital facility for POWs in the Philippines, all of the seriously injured POWs would be sent there. Many of the patients had grave injuries, often with missing limbs, terrible scars, and agonizing pain. POWs moved there from other camps were often shocked at the sight of so many badly injured POWs and found Bilibid more depressing than the other camps where they had been.

The prisoners had to show the guards respect at all times, saluting and bowing or risk being slapped or beaten. At times it didn't take anything to provoke a guard and often terrible cruelties would be inflicted upon the prisoners. It's been said that the guards generally came from the lowest levels of Japanese society or were Formosan conscripts, who the Japanese considered barely above the POWs. They were often insensitive to the suffering they inflicted on the prisoners. To make matters worse the prisoners had to deal with the tropical heat, mosquitos, and the monsoon rains that would periodically flood the prison camp.

While most of the surrendering forces on Corregidor were sent to prison camps shortly after their surrender in May, some of the men like Max continued to be held at Ft. Hughes and Corregidor for several additional months to serve the needs of the Japanese on these two islands. After being transferred from Ft. Hughes and Corregidor, Max was first sent to a prison camp at Cabanatuan for about a week before being sent to Bilibid where George was being held. It is likely that George and Max would have met before the war while both were assigned to the Canacao Navy Hospital. But their bond of friendship would certainly become much stronger while enduring the stress and abuses of their imprisonment. As corpsmen, George and Max worked with a team of American doctors at Bilibid performing a wide array of functions. Some of the medical staff at Bilibid would periodically be taken to other camps to take care of Americans who were in Japanese prison camps throughout the Philippines. While some corpsmen were used as laborers, it is believed that most if not all of George and Max's time was spent caring for the needs of the sick and injured at Bilibid before eventually being sent to Japan.

At Bilibid, Max recalled that as the war progressed *"We were [eventually] cut to two meals a day and we got the routine slapping or jabs in the chest with the butt of a Jap's rifle. The slaps didn't hurt much, but they made us mad. We hated to be slapped by a Jap who had to stand on his tiptoes to reach us."* Max remained in Bilibid with George for the next two years.

During the day many of the POWs at Bilibid, including corpsmen, who were not needed at the time for medical and administrative duties, were assigned to various work details such as working in the fields or as laborers on military construction projects. One of George's fellow prisoners and corpsmen, Ernest J. Irvin, had been assigned to the farm detail and commented *"On the farm we had to pull weeds with our right hand and place them in our left hand till it was full, then we had to lay the weeds in a circle around the crop plants for mulch. We were barefooted always and couldn't kneel, squat, sit or lie down, just bend at the waist – we called it the "head down ass up detail"."* Officers were not required to work on the farm except on a volunteer basis, but rather they were assigned administrative jobs. The medical officers and staff were generally assigned to the prison hospital under the direction of a Japanese doctor named Lieutenant N. Nogi. He had been a Seattle physician before the war and was generally considered to have been kind to the American prisoners and tried to abide by the Geneva Convention.

Brothers Born of Adversity

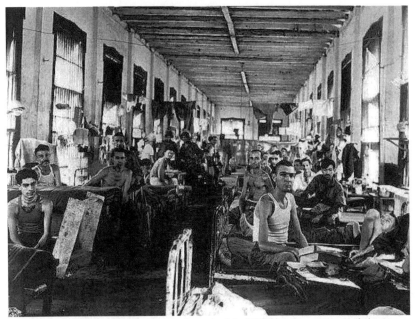

National Archive Photo. Scene from inside Bilibid Prison Hospital during WWII.

The prison administration allowed the prisoners to have religious services on Sunday, which provided so many of them a sense of hope and encouragement during such trying times. Several Navy and Marine chaplains were among the prisoners who would conduct the services and console the POWs. Their work was incredibly important since many of the POWs were becoming anxious and depressed from their long periods of captivity, the monotony, and constant harassment from the guards. Under such circumstances it was becoming easy for some of them to lose their will to live.

The POWs in the camps and in Bilibid would often pool their books to form a sort of library system that all the men could use. During those stressful times, it was said that the bibles placed in these libraries were constantly being read by someone. In addition to men's spiritual needs, it was important for the men to have a "buddy system," friends whom one could really trust and count on. Loners were always a target of the less scrupulous, whether from captor or fellow POW. It was common for men from the same town or state to find each other and to become

Brothers Born of Adversity

friends. George's hometown of Berry, Alabama was less than 60 miles from Max's hometown of Birmingham, Alabama, so it is easy to understand how and why they would have connected. There is a bible verse, Proverbs 18:24 that reads, *"A man of many companions may come to ruin, but there is a friend who sticks closer than a brother."* It is this kind of relationship that George and Max developed. They would always look out for one another through the times of adversity they shared and would become life-long friends and as close as brothers.

Most of the men's free time conversations were now primarily about food rather than women and sex. They would often share stories about back home or speculate about when they might be liberated. Some suggested that it also included some time for swapping lies. Lectures would be organized for the sake of helping to keep morale up. Often the lectures would be about food and recipes. For George, he would have surely remembered and spoken of his mother's cooking, and the smell of fresh cornbread and turnip greens cooking with ham on the stove and how the family would sit together on the front porch shelling beans. He would have also shared how his mother loved her rose garden and how she would often sing her favorite gospel hymn, "He Walks with Me" as she worked around her home and yard:

"I come to the garden alone, while the dew is still on the roses.
And the voice I hear falling on my ear, the Son of God discloses.
And he walks with me and he talks with me, and he tells me I am his own.
And the joy we share, as we tarry there, none other has ever known.
He speaks and the sound of his voice, is so sweet the birds hush their singing
And the melody that he gave to me, within my heart is ringing,
And he walks with me and he talks with me, and he tells me I am his own."

Years earlier George could not wait to get away from home, but now his heart yearned to be back home with his family. Max had similar memories to share about his mother and also missed home immensely.

Brothers Born of Adversity

For a time, the guards allowed the prison to have a store where the prisoners could sell things that the Japanese had not already taken from them. The officers were less likely to have had things like their rings and such confiscated than the enlisted men. Some of the men like Ted Lewin, who will be discussed in more detail later, still managed to have cash and/or connections on the outside to people who could get them money. According to the Geneva Convention, POWs were to be provided a certain amount of pay for their labor. Although the Japanese did not ratify the Geneva Convention, they claimed to be paying the men a wage for their labors. However, they reduced their pay for their food and other provisions, leaving the men next to nothing or nothing at all. This allowed the men who had money or items to trade to acquire food items such as canned meat and fish, but mostly items like beans, garlic, and bananas to add to a dish they referred to as *Quan*. This dish was generally shared among a group of POWs. On rare occasions the POWs were allowed to receive some of the Red Cross packages that had been sent from home. Often these packages would include canned fish and meat, which was considered a real prize. The men would hold on to such items as if it were a treasure. They would have to be careful to keep it concealed, so that it wouldn't be taken from them or stolen. Decades later, after George passed away, his family was surprised to find that George had several cans of sardines and potted meat hidden among his possessions; an apparent obsession that stuck with him from his years as a POW.

The medical staff was also able to trade some of their few medical supplies with the guards for food and cigarettes. Throughout the men's imprisonment a thriving black-market seemed to always exist, sometimes even involving the Japanese guards. One popular item desired by the Japanese soldiers was the drug sulfa; used to treat venereal disease, which was common among the Japanese soldiers. However, the camp's supply was quickly used up. In one camp, some unscrupulous, but enterprising prisoners had managed to create some fake sulfa from plaster, sugar, and water. They used an old spent bullet cartridge as a mold. This was then used to trade with the Japanese. While trading fake drugs would normally be deemed unethical, it is hard to pass judgement on men who were undernourished and just trying to survive.

Brothers Born of Adversity

One story told by a former POW at Bilibid recalled an incident in which a Japanese or Formosan guard urinated from an upstairs window or balcony onto the electric fence that surrounded the prison complex and was electrocuted. While many of the POWs found the incident amusing it was not something that could be joked about openly in front of the guards without being punished.

Most of the men had only one set of clothes to wear during their time at Bilibid which would eventually become torn and ragged. Other than a few blue dungarees from the American quartermaster depots, the men had to patch their clothing the best they could until what they wore was beyond repair. The Japanese provided some of the men a piece of cloth that they would wear as a G-string to keep them from going completely naked. Many of the men had no shoes to wear. Eventually the Japanese provided equipment for a cobbler's shop, but they did not provide sufficient materials to make all the men shoes.

Despite the conditions that George, Max, and the other corpsmen endured, they were a very well-respected group of men. In a memorandum dated May 17, 1944, the senior medical officer at Bilibid hospital, T. H. Hayes, states in part the following:

> "The maintenance of their unflagging spirit is reflected in the excellent calibre of their work in the presence of a woeful lack of facilities; in their uncomplaining acceptance of the misfortunes of war; the sustained high general tone of good order and discipline among them; their clean smart appearance in spite of the disheartening dearth of clothes; the wholesome hygienic condition in which I have always found their crude quarters."

While POW life in the prison camps seemed like hell, the men were not alone in their suffering. Families back home were also anxious and hurting, not knowing whether their loved ones were alive or dead; whether they were sick or well. Max's mother was a strong woman, but the stress of having her only son missing or imprisoned was immense. George's parents, like many parents of missing military personnel, contacted their local U.S. Congressman in an effort to learn any word of their son. Having their son missing and daughters now serving as nurses

Brothers Born of Adversity

in the U.S. Army brought a lot of stress on the family and more than likely contributed to George's father's declining health. Finally, at the end of April 1943 the Navy Department sent George's father a letter advising him that through the International Red Cross's efforts, they had learned through official Japanese sources that George was being held as a prisoner of war in the Philippine Islands. Knowing that George was alive brought some comfort but did not lessen their concern. A copy of the letter from the Navy Department follows:

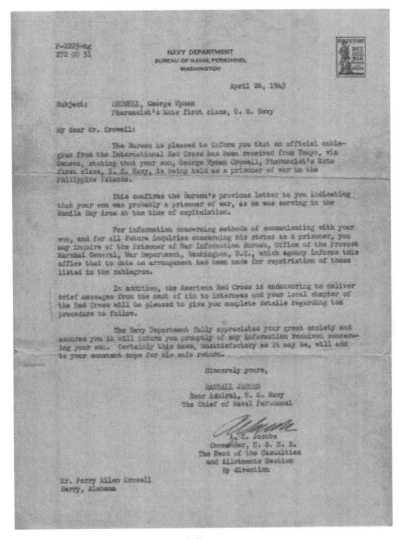

Brothers Born of Adversity

Also caught up in the war were many American civilians who had farming and other business interests in the Philippines. With the invasion of the Philippines, they too became prisoners of the Japanese Empire. It is interesting to note that some of these civilian women, although imprisoned, were allowed more freedom than the male and military prisoners. Some used this opportunity to raise funds from churches and other organizations and individuals to purchase food, clothing, and medicine to supplement the poor provisions that the military prisoners were being provided, even though they had inadequate provisions as well. In 1944, the Vatican was permitted to give each of the American prisoners being held in Bilibid a papal gift of 300 pesos. Additionally, many of the Filipino people would pass food or cigarettes to the prisoners when they had an opportunity. During the Bataan Death March, there were stories of Filipino women losing their lives for trying to provide the American and Filipino soldiers a little food or water along their march. It is often easy to overlook the valor and unselfish acts of such civilians in the midst of a brutal war, but often they too were just as heroic as those in military service.

One individual of some notoriety living in Manila prior to the war was an American civilian named Ted Lewin. In a 1959 article in Time Magazine, he was described as a rugged, soft-voiced, American ex-prizefighter with a taste for dark shirts, penthouses, air-conditioned Cadillacs, and shadowy wheelings and dealings. Other sources say he had mob connections in Chicago and may have had to flee the States for killing a man. Reporter and author, George Weller described him as *"a big broken-nosed soldier of fortune who had been a reporter in Los Angeles on the Huntington Park Record and proprietor of an offshore gambling ship."* Another source said he also operated illicit operations, such as prostitution, at the same time. It is said that he had come to the Philippines as a sports promoter and night club owner with intentions of also running illicit operations such as gambling and prostitution. It is hard to separate the truth from the myth of this man.

When the war started in the Philippines, Ted Lewin was supposedly commissioned into the army as an officer. One can only speculate whether his commission was official and for patriotic reasons or was done with the thought that he would fare better in a military officer's uniform.

Brothers Born of Adversity

After the fall of Bataan, he spent some time as a POW in Bilibid where George and Max were being held. He would also be among them on the *Oryoku Maru*, *Enoura Maru*, and *Brazil Maru*, as well as with them in the same prison camp in Japan. They would have most certainly had to know one another during this time. Interestingly, Ted Lewin is mentioned in many of the books written about the *Oryoku Maru* and the hell ship experience, although again, it is difficult to separate fact from myth. Several sources claimed that he had other POWs who served as his bodyguards while imprisoned and that he managed to get special favors from the Japanese for himself and his close associates. He also maintained close relationships with some of the senior POW officers.

The International Red Cross, headquartered in Switzerland, a neutral country during the war, played a critical role in delivering communications between prisoners of war and their families, both to the Allied and Axis powers. It also provided a means for families to send packages to the prisoners, as well as providing them other humanitarian aid such as food and medicine. However, not all the mail, packages, and aid went to where it was intended. The few Red Cross packages that the men did receive played a big, although temporary measure in improving the health and diet of the POWs and more than likely saved many of the men's lives. The International Committee of the YMCA, also based in Switzerland, played a key role in providing prisoners with spiritual, educational, and recreational resources, and a wide range of books that had been donated to the organization.

The Red Cross issued postcards to the prisoners that they could send to their families. However, the postcards were monitored by the Japanese military and provided little space or opportunity to give details of their imprisonment. Prisoners could not be candid about their health or condition for fear of retribution by the guards and also not wanting to worry family back home any more than necessary. Following is a copy of the front and back of one of the Red Cross postcards that George was able to send home to his mother.

Brothers Born of Adversity

Chapter 4 – Allied Forces Begin Invasion of the Philippines

The United States had been quick to mobilize for the war effort, preparing men, ships, planes, equipment, and supplies at an unprecedented level. The Allied nations had begun a long strategic move against Japan by island hopping and capturing one island base after another along the Japanese Empire's ever-shrinking perimeter. Submarines played a vital role in helping to defeat Japan by sinking its merchant ships, troop transports, and cutting off its much-needed oil supplies. It had become increasingly difficult for Japan to supply and maintain all of its far-reaching military bases across the Pacific. The Allies were steadily moving toward the Japanese mainland. The Japanese anticipated that there would be an Allied invasion of the Philippine Islands in the Leyte Gulf by the middle of 1944 and committed their remaining naval power in an all-out offensive to stop the invasion. The resulting Battle of Leyte Gulf was the largest naval battle in history and for the Japanese it was catastrophic, resulting in the greatest loss of men and ships in combat during the war. The liberation of the Philippines meant that Japan would be cut off from much needed oil and other resources from their occupied areas of Southeast Asia.

On October 20, 1944, American troops began their initial landing in the Philippines on Leyte Island, an island southeast of Luzon. They had hopes of taking Mindoro Island just south of Luzon by November 20, 1944, but this invasion was delayed until December 5th and then to December 15th. Had an earlier Allied invasion date of Mindoro occurred, it is unlikely that the *Oryoku Maru* would have been able to enter Manila Bay and load George, Max, and over 1,600 other POWs for transport to Japan on December 13, 1944. The Japanese still had 200,000 troops in the Philippines to try to withstand the American assault. On October 25th the Japanese commenced what they would call the kamikaze or "Divine Wind," which were suicide air attacks with one out of eight hitting their target. The Japanese believed that they had been saved twice from Mongol invasions centuries earlier when typhoons destroyed the Mongol invasion fleets and thus the belief that the "Divine Wind" or kamikaze would save them again. While ultimately the kamikaze did not save

Brothers Born of Adversity

Japan, they weren't without effect on America's amphibious invasions through the remainder of the war.

National Archive photo of General MacArthur wading ashore during the Leyte Gulf invasion to retake the Philippines in October 20, 1944, where he made his well-known "I have returned" speech.

George and Max, along with their fellow prisoners, although weak from decreased rations and disease, were hopeful that they might soon be liberated. By this time, Bilibid was busy as a clearinghouse for POWs as other prison camps on the islands were being closed and prisoners were being shipped off to Japan or elsewhere. By December 1944 the American forces were bombing targets in the Manila area, destroying many Japanese ships in Manila Bay, as well as targets near Bilibid. The POWs in Bilibid could watch the Japanese and Allied aircraft in "dog fights" overhead and hoped that they would soon be rescued. The commanding officers among the POWs convinced the Japanese to allow them to paint in large letters "PW" on the prison roofs to alert the Allies that the facility contained POWs and thus minimize the chances of it being bombed. Because of the role the medical officers and staff had in managing the prison hospital, they were some of the last POWs to be transferred from Bilibid.

Brothers Born of Adversity

The Japanese were using the POWs as much as possible to help build defenses around the Manila area in preparation for the invasion that they knew would soon arrive. Some of the jobs POWs were forced to perform were dangerous and contrary to the Geneva Convention. Like the U.S. military, the Japanese recognized the value of the Bataan peninsula as a strategic defensive location and hoped to supply it better than what MacArthur had been able to do before the Japanese invasion. They also began destroying anything that might be of value to the Allies when they returned, including the Manila Hotel where MacArthur had a suite years earlier, when he was living in the Philippines.

The POWs imprisoned in the Philippines had justified concerns that the Japanese could potentially have them killed before American forces arrived to liberate them. The massacre that occurred on Palawan Island is a chilling example of the Japanese "extreme measures." The Palawan Island is a long narrow island to the southwest of Manila. Under the pretext of an air raid the Japanese herded over 100 POWs into a tunnel with a single entrance that had been built along a beach area. Several of the men distrustful of the Japanese actions continued to burrow out onto an unguarded beach area to manage their escape as the Japanese deliberately torched the entrance of the tunnel; burning and suffocating the men inside. One source claimed that a POW who had been set ablaze ran out of the tunnel and grabbed a nearby Japanese soldier and dragged him back into the burning tunnel with him as a final act of revenge.

The Japanese had been shipping POWs off to Japan, Korea, and China for some time. Early in the war the Japanese controlled the shipping lanes in the Western Pacific and could transport prisoners, troops, and supplies with minimal risk. However, as the war progressed, Allied forces started taking a significant toll on Japanese shipping. Transports carrying prisoners of war were most often not identified by the Japanese as prison ships, while in other instances the Japanese had used Red Cross markings to conceal the fact that they were shipping military supplies for the war effort. By the beginning of December 1944, several Japanese ships transporting Allied prisoners had already been sunk by Allied aircraft and submarine personnel who were not aware that the ships contained Allied prisoners. Thousands of Allied POWs suffered this fate and the threat of it recurring increased with each passing day. It was also a terrifying experience for many of the Japanese sailors assigned to these transports and other naval vessels who were aware of the dangers. Many thousands of Japanese sailors would lose their lives as a result of Allied attacks on their ships.

As noted earlier, Bilibid served as a clearinghouse for POWs before shipping them out to Japan or elsewhere, as well as being the primary medical facility for sick and injured POWs in the Philippines. When new POWs were brought into Bilibid, they were often shocked by the sight of all the men who were legless, armless, or otherwise seriously injured or impaired. For George and Max, it was an everyday ordeal to care for and comfort these unfortunate souls. As new POWs were brought into Bilibid, new stories and rumors would circulate. One POW from Cabanatuan reported how the Japanese killed a POW for trying to escape. They had bashed his head in and gouged out his eyes. Then the body was carried through the POW shacks to show everyone what happens to those who try to escape. Another POW who had been in Cabanatuan recalled how the Japanese and Formosan guards had shown them a propaganda film he believed was made during the atrocities referred to as the "Rape of Nanjing". The film showed the Japanese soldiers throwing babies up in the air and catching them on bayonets. He said that the Japanese or Formosan guards who were showing them the film were laughing over it and that he would never understand the Japanese culture.

A group of English POWs was brought into Bilibid. They were bearded, dirty, emaciated, and covered with feces. They told how they had been kept in overcrowded holds of a ship with little food or water from Singapore or wherever before being brought to Bilibid. Despite their appearance, it was hard for the men to fathom such treatment until they were to experience it for themselves.

The Japanese were now in a rush to transport all remaining prisoners on the Philippine Islands that they deemed "fit to work" back to their homeland or other places where they needed laborers. Describing these sick and malnourished men as "fit to work" would have been laughable had it not been so tragic. But Japan needed manpower to supplement their diminished labor force resulting from the war effort. By the early

Brothers Born of Adversity

part of December 1944 there were approximately 2,000 prisoners left in Bilibid and about 25 percent were ill or patients in the hospital. The POWs had been hopeful that they would be rescued prior to being shipped off. They were well aware of the dangers of transport ships being sunk by American planes and submarines. The Japanese had been hindered from removing the remaining POWs due to the heavy air raids in and around Manila. Many Japanese ships caught in Manila Bay had already been destroyed. However, on November 28th the air raids suddenly stopped because of an unexpected typhoon, slowing the Allied advance and giving the Japanese an opportunity to bring their freighters back into the harbor.

On December 12th, the Japanese ordered an examination of all the prisoners to determine who was fit to be transported. The examination consisted of having each man walk into a room and around a chair. No questions were asked. It seemed being able to walk into the room and around a chair deemed the men fit enough to be transported. Some of the men left letters or wills with those prisoners who remained at Bilibid. Others chose to bury them in jars on the grounds of the prison compound in the belief that they would not survive. Now the only POWs that would be left at Bilibid were those with missing limbs, blind, or seriously ill. While one dark chapter in George and Max's prison experience was about to end, an even darker chapter was about to begin.

Brothers Born of Adversity

This photo illustrates how malnourished many of the POWs were, as well as how they were often dressed in what might be best described as G-strings, as a result of having a lack of adequate clothing. Public domain photo.

Chapter 5 - The *Oryoku Maru*

The *Oryoku Maru* sometime prior to being equipped for war.
Public domain photo.

In the early morning hours of December 13, 1944, 1,619 weak and ragged clothed POWs were ordered to prepare for a march to the waterfront docks on Manila Bay where they were to board a transport ship to Japan. The men had packed up their few belongings. They included their mess kits, an item they might have saved from one of their few Red Cross packages and/or anything they might have traded for or purchased. This morning they received their regular meal referred to as "lugao" or "lugau," but were given a double ration since it was to be the only meal they were to receive that day. The prisoners had not been limited on their water supply up to this point and were allowed to fill their canteens before leaving. The men were also issued a small ration of soap and toilet paper. The soap of course would not be of much use without sufficient water for bathing and the small amount of toilet paper would not be sufficient for such a long trip with men who would be suffering from diarrhea and the infectious disease dysentery. After having the men line up early for their march they were then told to wait. This delay gave the men hope that the voyage would be cancelled. But after several hours they were told to again prepare for the march. The men were broken up into three main groups under Lt. Colonel Beecher, Commander Portz, and Commander Josephs, and then into smaller groups of about 100.

The Japanese mainland needed laborers, and with Allied forces closing in on the Philippines, there was a rush to transport as many of the healthiest prisoners to the homeland as possible. The ones being moved on this day were the last of those that they deemed fit to work. Nearly two thirds of these prisoners were officers, including many doctors and chaplains, as well as many corpsmen like George and Max. Some of the enlisted men believed that the officers were protecting their own by allowing most of the enlisted men to be sent to Japan first. This could explain why so many officers were in the last groups to be shipped out. On the other hand, the Japanese were reluctant to assign officers to manual labor, so that could well have been a reason for shipping so many officers out last. Whatever the case, there were always rumors circulating, whether based on fact, fiction, hope, fear, or just entertainment.

Lieutenant Junsaburo Toshino, the Guard Commander, and his short hunchback interpreter Shusuke Wada, who insisted upon being called Mr. Wada, stood at the prison gate checking the number of prisoners as they passed them. Several of the men who were previously imprisoned at Davao POW Camp in the lower Philippines remembered Lieutenant Toshino from their imprisonment there and that he had vested much of his authority in Mr. Wada. They quickly surmised that Mr. Wada would again be the one who exerted control over them. Many of the men like George had been imprisoned in Manila since the city was initially surrendered nearly three years earlier. Others had been in different POW camps around the Philippines before being sent to Bilibid. Some of the prisoners had endured the Bataan Death March or, like Max, were among those forced to surrender with the fall of Corregidor. Included among the POWs were about 50 American civilians and 37 British and Dutch prisoners. While the men might have expected the trip to Japan to take a week or ten days, they had no way of knowing the horrors they were to experience on this trip that would take seven weeks. Had these men known what was in store for them they might have preferred to have been shot or stabbed to death rather than board the ship.

It was over a two-mile march from Bilibid to the docks where they were to be loaded on a transport ship. The men walked in ranks of four over the Quezon Bridge which crossed the Pasig River, then past the Philippine Legislative Building, around the old walled city, past the Manila Hotel, and then on to docks along the waterfront. Although weak from their poor diet, which had gotten worse as the war progressed, they were prodded along by bayonets and the clubs the Japanese referred to as "narugis." A truck followed the procession of POWs to pick up those who had fallen and who were too weak to continue the march. Sympathetic Filipinos gathered along the route to watch but were beaten back if they got too close to the prisoners. Occasionally the Filipinos would cautiously give a victory sign or turn up their radios for the men to hear as they passed. As the men trudged on, they witnessed the damage that had been done to the city since the start of the war.

At the waterfront, they were directed to Pier 7 which had been known as the "Million Dollar Pier." It was now badly damaged from Allied bombing as well as the earlier damage from the Japanese bombings. George and Max would have recalled first setting foot on the Philippine Islands at this very location, but everything was different now. There awaiting them was the *Oryoku Maru*. It was a large passenger cargo ship with several levels of cabins that had probably been designed for luxury travel in the Orient. Now it was outfitted with weapons and used for transport in the war effort. The remains of approximately 50 warships and freighters that had been sunk from Allied bombing could be seen in the harbor.

Beyond the *Oryoku Maru* were several other Japanese vessels which were intended to accompany her. Although already overheated, the prisoners were ordered to wait at the docks for several more hours while Japanese soldiers and equipment were unloaded. Then they waited for the boarding of passengers and the loading of supplies and large quantities of sugar. With the severe fuel shortages in Japan, sugar was being used to make ethanol as an alternative source of fuel. It was rumored that included in the cargo being loaded was General MacArthur's Packard automobile, a small trophy of their early success. About 700 well-dressed Japanese citizens, mostly women and children evacuees, boarded the ship to occupy the cabin space that was available. The overcrowded ship also carried approximately 1,000 Japanese seamen whose ships now lay sunken in Manila Harbor. Additionally, there were about 100 crew members and 30 Japanese and Formosan guards. While waiting at the pier, Mr. Wada placed Lt. Colonel Beecher in charge of the entire group of prisoners although Commander W. P. Portz was a few years his senior in rank. The Japanese Army and Navy were often at odds with one another. This may have played some role in their making Lt. Colonel Beecher, who was an army officer, in charge of the POWs, rather than Commander Portz, who was a naval officer.

After several hours the guards started loading the POWs into one of the three cargo holds on the ship under the watchful eye of Mr. Wada. The process of loading the POWs took several more hours. The guards filled the aft or stern of the ship first with over 800 men; mostly comprised of the highest-ranking American officers. Commander Portz was in charge of this group. The hold was very dark since someone had broken the electrical cable to the only light fixture in the hold. The hatch entrance to the aft hold had a canopy or platform built over it that further restricted light in the hold below. A long wooden narrow staircase led from the deck down into the hold 35 feet below. A double deck of stalls or bays had been built around the perimeter of the hold about three or four feet from the floor and nine feet deep. The men were forced to climb down into the dark hold where they were beaten and prodded to the back of the hold by the guards with the butts of rifles, broom handles, or the supervising Japanese officer's sword.

One particularly vicious guard, a Lance Corporal named Kazutane Aihara who the POWs had nicknamed "Air Raid," stood at one of the holds beating prisoners with his "narugi" club as they entered. He had already earned a reputation in the Cabanatuan prison camp for sneaking up on prisoners and beating them for no reason. Whenever he was spotted, someone would shout "Air Raid" to alert other POWs so they could try and get out of his way; thus, the reason for his nickname. Ted Lewin knew "Air Raid" well from having been in the Cabanatuan prison camp for over two years before being sent to Bilibid. While at Cabanatuan, Lewin managed to gain some favor with the guards by teaching them how to gamble. Many of his fellow POWs resented him for his cozy relationship with the Japanese and the fact that he had more resources to buy food and other items from the camp's black market. On the other hand, some of the senior officers would later find his ability to negotiate with and bribe their captors useful.

Brothers Born of Adversity

After being herded into the aft hold the POWs were required to sit either on the upper or lower level of the bays with their knees folded so that their backs were against the knees of the person behind them. The center of the hold was open, but so crowded that many men were forced to stand. In this overstuffed, hot, foul, and unventilated hold it became difficult for the men to breathe. Men quickly started fainting and fights began to break out as men panicked from the suffocating conditions.

Another 600 men were packed into the forward hold which had similar deplorable conditions as the aft hold. Lt. Col. Beecher was the senior officer in this group. George and Max, along with most of the medical personnel were among the remaining men forced into the hold that was amidships. This was the only hold that was fully ventilated. Commander Maurice Joses, a navy doctor, was senior officer in this hold. Sometime between 5 p.m. and 7 p.m. on December 13, 1944, the *Oryoku Maru* cast off from the pier, moving out of the bay and making anchorage near Corregidor for the remainder of the night.

Soon after being crammed into the holds, some of the men began suffocating from the lack of oxygen in the aft and forward holds where there was no ventilation. American officers directed that the men in the back of the hold who had passed out from lack of air be passed overhead by the others to the hatch area where the air was better. This saved several of the men's lives. Despite such heroic efforts, many men died the first night. Men screamed and begged for air and water almost non-stop. Commander Portz, who oversaw the men in the aft hold, became seriously ill. As a result, command was taken over by Commander Bridget who had been Max's commanding officer on Caballo.

Some of the POWs, including Ted Lewin, and very likely some of the corpsmen like George and Max, were used by the Japanese on food or work detail which gave them a chance to get out of the hold for a brief period. Before dark, buckets were lowered down to the men with some sort of rice mixture, as well as some empty buckets for toilet use. The distribution of the food and water was left up to the POWs and amounted to less than a canteen cup of steamed rice with salt and seaweed and about three teaspoon sips of water per man. Some of the men took more than their share, resulting in others going without anything to eat or drink. In the dark it was sometimes difficult for the men to distinguish one bucket from another. In their tortured state of mind some men would find humor in misleading their fellow prisoners as to the contents of buckets.

In the crowded, foul conditions, dysentery was quick to spread among the men and without adequate toilet facilities they generally had no choice but to relieve themselves right where they stood or lay. Desperate for anything to drink, some POWs would drink their own urine. Yet others, using knives or possibly sharp instruments they had handmade, slit the throats of those who had died in order to suck their blood. Others, seeing this, cut the throats of those nearby who might have simply fallen asleep. Some of the men tried to ration the remaining water in their canteens only to awaken to find that someone else had drunk what remained while they were asleep. Thievery would continue to be a problem as those so inclined or desperate preyed upon their fellow POWs. A sense of paranoia set in as men realized that in such dire circumstances, they didn't know who they could trust. Deranged men would scream or attempt to walk around in an aimless manner causing fights to break out. As one man was being stabbed by the man next to him, his cries for help were in vain since he could not be located in the dark. Conditions were somewhat better in the amidship hold where George and Max were, but they could hear the cries and screams coming from the aft hold.

It is difficult for a sane, rational, and charitable individual to fully comprehend the extent of the madness men were driven to in their efforts to survive as they struggled for air and fought for food and water. In G. Kurt Piehler's book, *A Religious History of the American GI in World War II*, he refers to a postwar memoir by James Stewart who survived the voyage. Stewart said that while he was able to retain his faith in God, his faith in man began to fail and he even began to doubt and fear his closest companion. He went on to say that he had witnessed several horrific incidents during the voyage, but one was especially tragic. Two West Point graduates, a father and son, had engaged in a fierce mortal combat. Piehler provides the following quote from Stewart: *"I remembered how they had protected and cared for each other in the years past…. The son*

Brothers Born of Adversity

was killing his father. I could see the look in the father's eye. A look of compassion and pity for the son who was a maniac."

Officers with the strongest constitutions and who were well respected by the men, like Commander Bridget, now the senior officer in the aft hold, and Lt. Colonel Beecher, senior officer in the forward hold, did their best to keep some semblance of order, while keeping the most deranged of their men under control. Providing leadership under such circumstances was difficult and it took more than mere rank to earn the respect and trust of the men.

Temperatures in the holds had gotten well over 100 degrees; particularly in the aft and forward holds. Men were becoming dehydrated as well as suffering from the lack of air. Commander Bridget and Lt. Colonel Beecher pleaded with Mr. Wada to move some of the men out to provide more air, as well as to provide water, but he refused. They also pleaded with Mr. Wada to let one very sick officer out of the hold to get some air to prevent him from dying from a severe asthma attack, but Mr. Wada's response was *"let him die."*

As a result of the heat and lack of fresh air and water, the noise and screams of the men grew worse. The POWs' screams and pleas were generally met by the guards responding with threats or hollering "Kora" at them, which is Japanese for keep quiet or shut up. Mr. Wada told the POWs that their screams and noise were disturbing the Japanese women and children above and if they didn't quiet down, he would close the hatch doors. Despite the dire consequences, the officers were unable to quiet the men in such suffocating and appalling conditions. So, Mr. Wada did as he promised and closed the hatch doors, making the conditions in the holds even more unbearable.

One former POW who had been transported on a different ship, but in similar circumstances, reported that some men who had been driven almost to madness resorted to cannibalism. Order was finally restored after the more rational men court martialed and hanged several of the offenders. The ship upon which these events occurred was not identified.

Brothers Born of Adversity

Men who had gone mad would often wander around aimlessly. In the aft hold, the most violently deranged men were placed in a sub-hold in the bilge area. Even some of the more mentally strong individuals reached their breaking point and committed suicide or as some of the men would say *"they took the short way home."* Gradually, exhaustion and threats by Mr. Wada to have the guards fire their guns into the holds seemed to settle the men down. During the first night approximately 50 men died. Despite the numerous horrors that George would endure during his imprisonment, the feeling of being stacked in the holds like logs remained the most vividly horrifying to him for the rest of his life.

Very early on the morning of December 14, 1944, the *Oryoku Maru* cast off again and joined a convoy of five merchant ships protected by some Japanese military destroyers and other navy ships. The convoy made its way north along the Bataan coast near Subic Bay. By this time, many of the men in the back of the holds were unconscious from lack of air and dehydration despite the officers' efforts to help as many as they could. Commander Bridget and Lt. Colonel Beecher had taken positions at the tops of the stairs in their respective holds continuing to plea to the guards and Mr. Wada for relief. Finally, Mr. Wada reluctantly agreed to provide some water to these men and allow them to bring up their dead who had been stacked under the hatch door. He also finally agreed to allow some of the unconscious men to be brought up on the deck to try to revive them. After they were revived, they had to go back into the hold and a few more men were allowed to be brought up.

As the sun was rising, the guards, using POWs for the task, started providing some wooden buckets of rice to the prisoners. However, as the rice was being provided to those in the amidships hold, an air attack began as six American aircraft from the carrier USS *Hornet* attacked from the rear starboard side of the ship. The distribution of rice stopped, resulting in those in the forward and aft holds not being given any food all day. The POWs on the food detail were rushed back into their hold, but not before witnessing the commencement of the air attack and seeing one of the accompanying big ships in flames. The prisoners in the holds could hear the commotion on deck and the sound of anti-aircraft fire as wave after wave of air attacks continued. During the night, some of the POWs had crept up the staircases and had forced small openings

Brothers Born of Adversity

in the hatch planking to allow air in. After hearing the anti-aircraft fire and the strafing of bullets and the rockets from the American planes overhead, officers on the stairs would peek through the cracks and announce to the men what they could see happening.

The *Oryoku Maru* and the accompanying ships were strafed with bullets from the American aircrafts' wing-mounted machine guns and took hits from rocket fire as well. Some of the ships were now in flames or attempting to escape. The coal depot of the *Oryoku Maru* was now on fire. At this point the Captain of the *Oryoku Maru* decided to run the ship upon the shoals near the entrance to Subic Bay, which lay on the north side of the Bataan Peninsula. By running the ship upon the shoals, the captain hoped to keep the ship from sinking into the deeper water. American pilots making the attack had no way of knowing that the ship contained Allied POWs since the ship had not been properly marked.

Air attacks continued throughout the day, joined by additional American aircraft. The *Oryoku Maru* was hit by a 500-pound bomb on the port bow and another bomb to the cabin area. More fires began to break out on the ship. The ship's gunners destroyed several of the American aircraft before their main anti-aircraft gun malfunctioned and became unusable. The engine was also damaged which left the ship stranded on the shoal as the crew frantically attempted repairs. During the worst of the bombing, chaplains would stand and offer prayers for the men to be spared and, if not, to be given courage to die like men. The Japanese passengers and guards above deck were hit hard and their blood ran into the holds below, dripping on the men. Below deck, prisoners were also hit by bullets, shrapnel, or falling debris. In the amidship hold, the hatch cover was blown loose and came crashing down on the men below, killing and wounding many of the men. George was one of the wounded, suffering three large gashes to his midback. While the injuries George received were not immediately life threatening, they were painful and subject to infection, particularly due to the filthy conditions and the lack of proper medicine. Max did his best to stop the bleeding on George's back and clean and bandage the wounds. Then both he and George tended to the injuries of the other men. After the war, George would receive a Purple Heart Medal for the wounds he suffered while on the *Oryoku Maru*.

Brothers Born of Adversity

Holes created in the deck and bulkhead during the attacks provided some light and air into the dark holds. Some of the medical staff were called above deck to help with the wounded, which included many of the Japanese women and children. One surviving POW recalled that while waiting to board the *Oryoku Maru*, a young Japanese child who was boarding the ship with his mother, innocently waved at the POWs in a friendly manner. Now, even amidst his own suffering, he couldn't help but wonder if that innocent child and his mother were among those lying dead on the deck of the ship. It did not take long for some of the guards to begin venting their anger at the American medical staff who were trying to help. They began beating them and driving them back into the hold.

By late afternoon of December 14th, the engine on the *Oryoku Maru* had been repaired and high tide had lifted the ship off of the shoal. The damaged ship then limped along into Subic Bay where it made anchor a couple hundred yards off the former U.S. Navy base at Olongapo, which was now under the control of and being used by the Japanese. Mr. Wada advised the POWs that the Japanese nationals would disembark first and then the POWs would be allowed to disembark. It was close to midnight before the last of the Japanese nationals had been evacuated by lifeboats.

Conditions in the holds the second night were just as bad, if not worse than the first night. Men were now not only suffering from the heat and suffocation and lack of food and water, but many had painful wounds, and more were becoming deranged. Many men were howling and shouting. In Ted Lewin's testimony after the war, he recalled a deranged man trying to bite off his thumb. He was able to temporarily knock the man out, but ultimately the men around him killed him since there was no hope to quiet him. Many believed that Lewin had fellow POWs that served as his personal bodyguards while he was a POW himself. So, it is very possible that the men who killed the individual who tried to bite off Ted Lewin's thumb were those who served in this capacity.

Officers continued to plead with the men to settle down. Some of the chaplains tried to quiet and comfort the men by reading from their bibles and offering prayers for deliverance. At this point there was not much else they could do as they waited and wondered if they might die at any moment in another air or submarine attack before being unloaded. They were also aware of the possibility that the Japanese might not have any real intentions of allowing them to disembark before the American airplanes returned to finish sinking the *Oryoku Maru*. It was estimated that another 60 to 80 POWs died this day.

In the early hours of the morning of December 15, 1944, Mr. Wada told the men in the holds that they would shortly be allowed to evacuate from the ship after Japanese soldiers were in place to keep anyone from escaping. He instructed them to remove their shoes since they would have to swim, but it was also a way to minimize the chances of them escaping. As a result of the heat, many of the men had taken off most of their clothing and were now only wearing what might be described as G-strings - pieces of clothing they used to cover their genital area. The guards were instructed to shoot any POW whenever deemed necessary.

Before the men were allowed out of the holds another air raid by American planes commenced. This time the *Oryoku Maru* experienced a direct hit in the aft or rear hold killing a few hundred of the POWs and creating a hole in the side of the ship. Some of the men used this opportunity to try to escape, but only one or possibly two were known to have been successful in his efforts. Those caught attempting to escape were quickly shot. The one known POW who was successful in escaping used an overturned wooden crate that he found floating in the water. He slipped under it and waited for the opportune time to push toward the shore on the other side of the bay. There he was assisted by some friendly Filipinos and, with the help of their guerilla forces, he managed to reach the American invasion forces safely.

Another bomb hit the forward section of the ship, killing and wounding men in the forward hold. Wounded men and dead bodies seemed to be everywhere. As the holds filled with yellow smoke and noxious fumes from the bomb blasts, men frantically began trying to get out of the damaged holds. In the confusion, some guards shot into the hold and others threw grenades in the hold to stop the prisoners from coming out. By this time, whether directed to or not, the POWs were now crawling out of the holds. One young, scared guard dropped his rifle as he jumped back from the men coming out of the hold. One of the POWs cautiously picked up the gun, turned the barrel around toward himself, and handed it back to the guard in a nonthreatening manner to keep it from being the cause of the guards opening fire on them.

George and Max stayed close together so they would not get separated. Men looked to each other for help and support, since they were not sure who else they could rely on. This buddy system was instrumental in their survival. George, Max, and several other POWs managed to get above deck and started scavenging around for what they might find on the ship. Drinking water was the most desperately needed item at this time. In their search the men found bags of sugar and Red Cross packages with canned meat and cheese which they hurriedly tried to eat or carry with them. Some of the Red Cross packages contained much needed medicine, which Max and others decided to try and carry with them. George grabbed a couple of cans of potted meat for himself and Max. However, some of the Japanese officers were still on board doing some scavenging of their own and shot at any POW they found doing the same. One former POW recalled seeing a friend sitting in the galley area eating some food he had found when Lt. Toshino walked in with his pistol drawn and shot him dead.

After getting back out on the deck George and Max began helping those who needed assistance. For corpsmen like George and Max it had become second nature to assist the weak and injured, even when their own lives were in danger. POWs too weak to swim were helped into a lifeboat. Unfortunately, the lifeboat was soon strafed with bullets from the American airplanes' machine gun fire. No life vests or life belts were provided to the POWs, so George, Max and others would remove those found on dead Japanese and place them on the weakest prisoners or those unable to swim. Pieces of planking and floating debris would also be used as flotation devices.

The *Oryoku Maru* was now on fire and filling with smoke and the American airplanes were returning. As the ship continued to burn, ammunition that was stored on board started to explode. Shin Kajiyama, the Japanese Captain of the ship, urged the men on deck in his broken English to get off the ship before it completely blew-up and sank. There was now a mad rush to abandon ship and start swimming for shore. As the POWs swam to shore there were still wounded men in the holds whom no one was able to rescue.

National Archive photo. This incredible picture is an aerial photo actually showing the bombing of the *Oryoku Maru*, with POWs swimming away from the ship.

Jumping into the cool water initially felt refreshing and seemed to give the POWs a renewed sense of energy. Although the salt water burned the open wounds on George's back, he seemed to hardly notice with all that was happening around him. By this time the water was littered with debris, dead bodies and POWs trying to tread water or swim to shore. As the American airplanes began another dive towards them, George and

Brothers Born of Adversity

Max used bodies that were floating in the water to give themselves some protection from the strafing of machine gun fire.

As they encountered fellow POWs struggling in the water, George and Max would attempt to assist them onto floating debris so they wouldn't drown. In some cases, they would swim up to a struggling man from behind, grabbing him around the neck and armpit to avoid being pulled underwater and drowned. After securing these men, they would begin scissor kicking toward shore.

The scene was horrific above the water, but another threat lurked in the water as sharks that had been attracted by the blood circled. If these perils were not enough, the Japanese had set up machine guns along the shoreline and would fire across the water to discourage POWs from attempting to escape. As POWs intentionally or unintentionally swam or drifted off course there was no reluctance by the Japanese to open fire on them. Many of the men died trying to get to shore. Many more would have died if not for the brave, unselfish efforts of POWs like George and Max.

Along the shore was an eight-foot sea wall where the water was ankle-deep. After reaching the shoreline, some POWs not realizing they were required to stay in the water, were shot as they attempted to pull themselves over the top of the sea wall. The POWs had to stay in the shallow water along the sea wall until they were told they could come out. Lt. Colonel Beecher took quick command at the sea wall by directing additional men to swim back out to help those who were still struggling to swim to shore, as George, Max, and several others were already doing. POWs making it into the shallow water near shore began waving their arms at the American planes overhead in hopes that they would recognize them as prisoners of war. Their efforts seemed to have paid off as the American pilots wagged the wings of their planes and ended their attack.

In one direction the POWs waiting in the shallow water could see the cliffs of Bataan and in another direction, they could see the old navy yard near the town of Olongapo. While the ocean water initially felt invigorating to the weak and dehydrated men, it was soon causing chills

Brothers Born of Adversity

in the weakened men as they waited in the water. Eventually Lt. Colonel Beecher was able to negotiate with the Japanese to allow the men to get out of the water and warm themselves in the sun. Since the prisoners had little or no water to drink in two days, they pleaded with their captors to allow them to get some water to drink from a nearby water faucet, which the Japanese reluctantly allowed them to do in groups of five. As the men were coming ashore, Japanese guards attempted to search them for any contraband the POWs might have taken from the ship. George and Max and the others who had managed to scavenge some food and medicine from the ship had to hide the items in what little clothing they had.

The prisoners were then marched to the old navy base where they waited again until the Japanese decided what to do with them. It was eventually decided that they would be moved to a set of double tennis courts on the base. The tennis courts were surrounded by a short wall with a chicken wire fence above it. The two adjoining tennis courts provided little space to accommodate the number of POWs that were being placed there but would serve as their new prison camp for the next five or six days. With nearly 1,300 surviving POWs, the crowded tennis courts offered little space for the men to lie down or to stretch out. Lt. Colonel Beecher took position in the raised referee's chair or platform at the tennis courts and attempted to keep order among the unruly men. The guards called rosters several times to determine the number of survivors. A small area was set aside as a hospital where the sick and wounded could be cared for by the medical doctors and corpsmen. Two sheets and some raincoats were stretched over this area to give the sick and injured some protection from the sun. Among the medicine that Max had been able to secure from the Red Cross packages was a small bottle of Merthiolate, which he used to apply to the wounds on George's back to minimize the chances of infection. George would credit Max with saving his life; for without this medicine there would have been a high chance that his wounds would have gotten infected.

During this period one unfortunate incident involved a young POW whose arm was nearly severed during the attack on the ship. Believing their only chance in saving him was to amputate his arm, the medical staff did so, using only a pocketknife or razor blade (depending upon sources),

74

with no anesthetic, and limited medical supplies. Despite their best efforts, the patient died within a few days.

Later in the afternoon on December 15th the American pilots completed the destruction of the *Oryoku Maru* and bombed some of the military installations in the area. The Japanese and Formosan guards believed that the American pilots knew that there were POWs on the tennis courts, so they stayed close by, believing it to be the safest place to be during the air raids. No food was provided to the POWs that day or the following day, December 16th. Mr. Wada claimed that because of jurisdictional issues he was having trouble getting food for his own guards, let alone the POWs. On December 17th, a small supply of Filipino-sized clothes was brought in by the Japanese and distributed to some of the men who were naked or near so. That evening the POWs were given one sack of uncooked rice to divide among themselves, which amounted to about two tablespoons full of the uncooked rice for each of the men. The same amount was provided on the 18th and 19th. On the 20th the ration of uncooked rice was increased to four tablespoons per man. One former POW remembered there being a four-foot-wide strip of grass between the courts upon their arrival. But soon thereafter, not a single blade of grass was left as the starving POWs quickly devoured any green edible plant they could find.

The POWs were allowed to dig a squat trench near the tennis courts for use by the men to relieve themselves. While being confined to the tennis courts there was little protection from the heat of the sun during the day or the cold at night. At this point the men had little clothing to wear. At night the men lay close to one another, which provided some warmth, but it was primarily necessitated due to the shortage of space. Several additional men died while at the tennis courts. The dead were stripped of their clothing so that others could use whatever they had. Although the POWs were weak from their poor diet, illnesses, and injuries, many of them still volunteered to help bury their dead. This gave them an opportunity to eat edible plants along the way including grass and leaves. Despite the hardships at the tennis courts, the men realized that, if the *Oryoku Maru* had not been sunk, few, if any of them would have survived the trip to Japan. They were now hopeful again that the delay would allow them time to be rescued by Allied forces.

Brothers Born of Adversity

After spending five days and nights at the tennis courts, the next segment of their journey was about to begin.

Brothers Born of Adversity

Chapter 6 - The Journey Across Luzon

On the afternoon of December 20, 1944, about half of the POWs were taken by trucks to San Fernando, Pampanga, which was only a little over 40 miles from Bilibid Prison in Manila. The next day the remaining POWs were transported there as well. Whenever American planes were heard overhead the trucks transporting the POWs would take refuge under trees along the road. At San Fernando, Pampanga, the first group of POWs was housed in a provincial jail which did not provide adequate space for the number of men imprisoned there. In the courtyard of the camp was a lemon tree that had all of its leaves plucked and eaten by the POWs shortly after their arrival. The second group was taken to an old movie theater where the Japanese felt they could securely house them until they moved them to their next location. While the movie theater was crowded and did not provide them with much space for sleeping, it did provide protection from the sun and from the cold at night. After their arrival, the POWs were provided some cooked rice delivered on sheets of corrugated metal roofing material and were allowed to get water from a spigot. They were also provided a few of the Red Cross packages brought along from Manila, which contained some much-needed medicine.

During the evening of December 23rd, in what seemed like a surprise show of compassion, Mr. Wada and some of the guards met with Lt. Colonel Beecher, informing him that they would transport some of sickest and most physically impaired prisoners back to Bilibid in Manila where they could get better care. Fifteen or 16 of the men were selected. According to one former POW, one of the healthier prisoners somehow managed to convince the officers that he was sick and needed to go as well. It was later learned that instead of transporting these men back to Bilibid, they were taken to a cemetery nearby where they were taken from the truck one at a time to a large hole that had been dug in the ground. There they were told to take a position as if they were in prayer and then were stabbed and beheaded. After the war, Lt. Toshino, who oversaw the executions, and several of the other participants, including the one nicknamed "Air Raid", were hung for this and other atrocities. Mr. Wada, who was also involved, received a life sentence but was released after serving only eight years. Appendix A provides additional details on the related war crime trials.

Brothers Born of Adversity

Execution of POW by Japanese soldier. Public domain
photo compliments of the Roger Mansell website titled,
Center for Research: Allied POWS Under the Japanese.

Early on the morning of December 24th the two groups of prisoners were joined together and marched to a railroad yard and then transported by train to San Fernando, La Union, a shipping port on the Lingayen Gulf. The prisoners were crowded into the small box cars and many injured prisoners and medical personnel were placed on top of the box cars in hopes that the American pilots flying overhead would realize that POWs were on the train. Of course, the Japanese were probably more concerned about protecting themselves and the military supplies stored onboard rather than the POWs. American and Japanese planes were periodically seen overhead in dogfights, but the train was not attacked. Along the way they passed a recently bombed rail yard with boxcars still smoldering. It was a stark reminder of the danger this trip entailed. As the train stopped or slowed down going through some of the small villages along the way, some of the Filipino civilians tossed fruit and eggs to those riding on top of the cars and the youth would shout *"Merry Christmas Joe"* in their Filipino accent. Inside the cramped box cars some of the POWs began fainting from the heat and lack of air and POWs would wave pieces of their clothing to help circulate the air in the overcrowded cars. Because of the crowded conditions, men suffering from diarrhea and dysentery had little choice but to defecate right where they stood.

One of the small railroad box cars used in the Philippines to transport POWs during WWII. Photo provided courtesy of the National American Defenders of Bataan and Corregidor Museum and Research Center. Photo credit: Fred Baldassarre.

After about a 14 to 18-hour trip, the train arrived at San Fernando, La Union early on a bitter cold Christmas morning. From the railroad station the POWs were marched to a schoolhouse about a mile away where Mr. Wada said water would be available. After arriving at the school, they learned that the well was about 100 yards away near a dwelling that was currently occupied by Japanese soldiers. The well was a typical Filipino shallow well and no more than 10 feet away from a latrine used by the Japanese soldiers. The POWs had to dig out the well about another five feet deep to get the promised water. The medical staff asked Mr. Wada for iodine to purify the water before the men were allowed to drink from it, which he provided. As some of the men were digging the well out, others were stripping a hibiscus bush to eat its leaves, along with some pigweed they found; anything that might provide a little nourishment. After the men had a chance to drink some water, they were again lined up and marched three miles on a coral shell road to an area of beach along the Lingayen Gulf where they would spend the next two days and nights. Most of the men were barefoot, so marching on the sharp coral shells to the beach was extremely painful to their feet. The nights were cold and windy, so they dug holes in the sand on the beach and huddled together, but they still shivered and shook from the cold. By midmorning the heat was intense and there was nothing to provide them shade. The men's skin blistered from the prolonged exposure in the sun, and they continued to grow weaker from near starvation, exhaustion, and exposure to the elements. Many were sick or injured and death among the POWs became routine.

In the morning a truck arrived with food, but no water. The guards had provided just enough rice balls so that each man could get one but, due to the breakdown of discipline, some men got two and others none. To help the men cool down the officers convinced the guards to let the men take turns going into the gulf to bathe. The guards agreed to allow groups of about 100 at a time to spend 10 minutes each bathing in the water. Some of the men were so dehydrated and thirsty that they attempted to drink the salt water and had to be pulled out of the water. For most of the POWs their responsibility was simply to obey orders and try to survive. However, the officers, medical staff, corpsmen, and chaplains who were still physically able, had a responsibility to care for the needs of their fellow POWs. Later that day water finally arrived, but the men were only provided one canteen cup full for every 20 men, which amounted to about a spoonful or so per man. After dark the men were provided with enough rice balls for one per man, but again, some got two and others none. Water was again provided, but this time a half canteen cup per man.

During one of Mr. Wada's inspections, he warned the men with a sadistic grin that they were sitting on drums of gasoline stored under the sand, so they had better hope that they don't get attacked by American aircraft. Although the men doubted him, in reality a large number of drums of gasoline were buried beneath them. With the POWs sitting above the stored gasoline, the Japanese thought it was less likely that American aircraft pilots would target the area and destroy their valuable gasoline. As the prisoners waited, the Japanese were busy unloading equipment and supplies from the ships anchored in the harbor. Near dark a group of Japanese soldiers drove up and began digging up the drums of gasoline that had been stored at the beach.

Before the war some of the men might have visited this area and remembered walking along the beach and enjoying its beauty and its peaceful setting, but war had changed all that. It was no longer viewed as a paradise to the men sitting there.

About 65 of the men had died since their arrival at San Fernando, La Union, bringing their number down to 1,234 from the initial 1,619 that began the voyage. Once again, any hope of being rescued before being shipped off to Japan was quickly fading.

Less than two weeks after the POWs were shipped off from the Lingayen Gulf area, Allied forces would land there.

Brothers Born of Adversity

National Archive map of the Philippines in 1944. Route added by author showing approximate route George, Max, and their fellow POWs were taken from Manila to Subic Bay, where the *Oryoku Maru* was sunk, and then across western Luzon to Lingayen Gulf, where the POWs boarded the *Enoura Maru* and the *Brazil Maru* for transport to Japan.

Brothers Born of Adversity

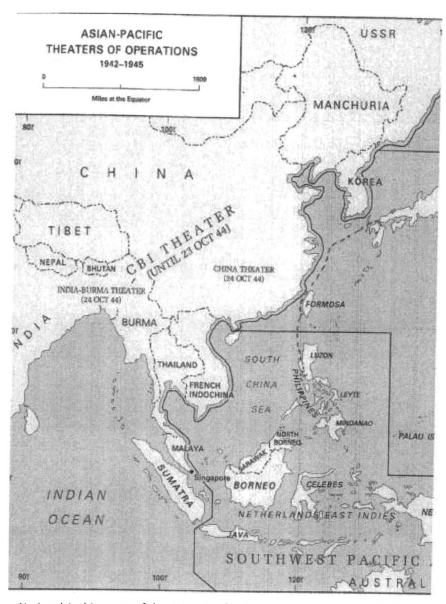

National Archive map of the Asian-Pacific Theater of Operations 1942-1945. Approximate route George, Max, and their fellow POWs were taken from the Philippines to Japan added by author.

Brothers Born of Adversity

Chapter 7 - The *Enoura Maru* and *Brazil Maru*

During the early hours of December 27, 1944, Lt. Toshino and Mr. Wada ordered the weak and weary POWs to line up and prepare to move out. From the beach area, the men walked north across the narrow isthmus of Poro Point to a partially protected bay and down toward two parallel wooden docks or piers. Out in the bay were about a half dozen Japanese freighters waiting, as well as the remains of several sunken ships. The men were herded onto the docks in the dark where they were to be loaded on barges, which would transport them out to two of the freighters awaiting them in the bay. As the men were lined up on the docks, some of the men took advantage of the darkness to plunder through some of the military food and supplies that had been stacked there.

The Japanese were in a big hurry on this morning and hastened the men along shouting *"speedo, speedo!."* Once the men were in the right position, they were ordered to jump on to the barges, which were some distance below. If a man hesitated when it was his turn to jump, a guard would push him off the dock. Several of the men were injured from the fall. One man missed the barge completely and hit his head on the side of the barge. Several of the men pulled him out of the water only to find that he had already died from his injuries.

Once they got to the freighters, the men with their blistered and cut feet were ordered to climb the rope ladders hanging from the sides of the ships. Under normal conditions this would not have been much of a challenge for most of the men, but in their weakened, sick, and injured condition it was a struggle for them to climb the ladders to board the freighters.

The awaiting freighters were only marked as Number 1 and Number 2, but they would later learn that they were named the *Enoura Maru* and the *Brazil Maru*. Like the *Oryoku Maru*, they contained no markings that would alert American pilots that they were transporting prisoners of war. The first 1,000 prisoners were loaded on the *Enoura Maru*, the largest of the two ships with Lt. Colonel Beecher in charge of the group. The remaining 234 prisoners which included George, Max, and Ted Lewin,

Brothers Born of Adversity

were loaded on the *Brazil Maru*. This ship was also transporting Japanese soldiers, some of whom were sick or injured. An officer named Johnson was in charge of this group of POWs.

The POWs were finally all loaded as the morning sun was rising and the ships were quickly underway. Those placed on the *Enoura Maru* were herded immediately down to the amidships hold which contained two levels and a floor that was about 60 feet square. While crowded, the conditions were much better for the men than on the *Oryoku Maru*. Those on the *Brazil Maru* were divided into several groups on deck while some of them were sent down in the hold to clean it before the rest were herded down there. The hold had contained horses and the smell of their excrement was overpowering, but it did not stop some of the starving men from eating kernels of corn that they found in the horses' manure. The horses' urine was being stored in the bilge area for later use in the production of explosives by the Japanese. The smell was nauseating and attracted horse flies, which constantly bit at the men. The POWs on both ships were again becoming desperate for water to the point that some would attempt to lick the condensation off pipes, only to be beaten by the guards if caught.

The *Enoura Maru*. Public domain photo.

Brothers Born of Adversity

While the prisoners had more room on these two ships than the *Oryoku Maru*, food was scarce, particularly on the *Brazil Maru*. On the *Enoura Maru*, the POWs' commanding officers had to plead with Lt. Toshino and Mr. Wada before they received any food and water. Later buckets of rice were lowered down to the men and water was provided. Since there was a limited number of buckets, the guards would not allow them to be kept down in the hold, so prisoners had to dump the rice on whatever they could find or directly onto the filthy floor. The ration amounted to about one mess kit of rice for every three POWs. On the fourth day no food was provided while on the fifth day they were provided some moldy rolls or biscuits that contained maggots. The medical staff designated the upper level in the hold of the *Enoura Maru* as the sick bay and attempted to organize the men for purposes of better distribution of food and such.

On the *Brazil Maru* the POWs were not issued food for the first two days except some of the leftover scraps from the guards. The guards would urinate on the scraps of food before tossing it to the starving POWs and then laugh as the prisoners scrambled and fought over it. George found it hard to forget or forgive such indignities that they were forced to endure. Only about two canteen cups of rice were provided to each of the men during their six-day voyage. Although the men in the *Brazil Maru* had attempted to clean up their hold the best they could, they continued to be plagued by biting horse flies for the duration of the voyage.

The *Brazil Maru*, most likely taken before being outfitted for war.
Public domain photo.

Brothers Born of Adversity

Moving north along the Luzon coast, both ships were spotted by a U.S. submarine which quickly and quietly moved into position to attack. After setting the *Enoura Maru* in its sights, it fired two torpedoes at the ship. Once the torpedoes were spotted, the captain and crew took quick evasive action and watched the torpedoes narrowly miss their ship and explode on the Luzon coastline.

As the ships moved northward, the temperature continued to drop and the prisoners continued dying from dehydration, starvation, and disease. On the *Enoura Maru* the sick bay on the upper level of the hold eventually became so overcrowded that some men would roll off the upper deck onto the lower deck, suffering severe injury and even death from the fall. Again, clothing was stripped from the dead to be used by the living.

As the deaths continued, Mr. Wada ordered that the dead be piled up in stacks of eight before they would be removed from the hold and tossed into the ocean. The corpsmen and chaplains who were still able continued to provide whatever comfort they could to the dying men. Religious rites were not allowed by the Japanese as the corpsmen tossed the dead overboard to be buried at sea. The lack of adequate food and water was the primary reason for so many deaths. When an officer among the POWs complained to the commander of the guards that, without more food and water, his men would die, he received the reply, *"We want you to die. Your submarines are sinking our ships."* One evening before reaching Takao, Formosa, food was sent down into the hold of the *Enoura Maru* in the dark. A food riot broke out as the starving men fought for some of the rice and spilled over a bucket of soup that had been provided. The riot went on for several hours until the men became too exhausted to continue.

Despite periodic attacks and damage done to the ships by American aircraft and submarines, the *Enoura Maru* and *Brazil Maru* arrived at the coast of Takao, on the western side of the island of Formosa on January 1, 1945. New Year's Day was the most important holiday to the Japanese and was celebrated from January 1st to the 4th. The holiday didn't mean much to the POWs, except that they saw less of the guards. On the *Brazil Maru* the men were surprised when the guards brought down a sack of a

Brothers Born of Adversity

hard bread, enough for five pieces for each man. This was the first bread that they had in a couple of years and the biggest meal since their journey had begun.

Upon their arrival at Takao, the prisoner count was down to about 1,150 from the original 1,619 that began the voyage. However, deaths would soon increase in much greater numbers. The men had lost significant amounts of weight and were now the weakest and most exhausted that they had been since their imprisonment started. While the ships were sitting in Takao harbor, the men in the holds could hear American and Japanese airplanes in dogfights overhead and prayed that they would not be bombed and shot at again.

Max recalled how he had been at a point of just giving up but had been encouraged by George. He would tell him that after the war he wanted him to visit him in Berry, Alabama and meet his five beautiful sisters. Sometimes the right words at the right time would give one the strength to carry on another day. George and Max would spend a considerable amount of time talking about their families. Max enjoyed hearing George talk about his sisters and by this time he must have felt like he knew them on a personal basis. George thought highly of Max and knew he would be proud to have him as a brother-in-law if they survived. Likewise, Max loved George like a brother and the idea of meeting George's sisters appealed to him. Such talks provided a necessary diversion from the hell hole they were in.

Some time on or before January 8, 1945, the Japanese transferred the remaining prisoners being held on the *Brazil Maru* to the forward hold of the *Enoura Maru*. At this point, all the surviving POWs were now on the *Enoura Maru*. Like the hold in the *Brazil Maru*, the forward hold on *Enoura Maru* had been used for transporting horses. Additionally, the POWs in the lower level of the amidships hold were moved out so that more bags of sugar in rice straw sacks could be stored there. These men were transferred to either the upper level of the same amidship hold or to the forward hold with the men from the *Brazil Maru*. This created much more crowded conditions for the POWs. At this time, most of the remaining British and Dutch prisoners were removed from the ship;

presumably to join others of their nationality being held in a camp on Formosa.

While the *Enoura Maru* was anchored in the harbor, another Japanese ship arrived and tied up next to it making both ships a more attractive target. On the morning of January 9, 1945, the American bombers attacked again, this time hitting the *Enoura Maru*. As before, the American airmen were not aware that the ship contained POWs. The first bomb hit the side of the ship near the forward hold, followed by two or three more bombs hitting directly on the deck. The explosions caused the ship to shake violently and tossed the POWs around. The bombs tore holes between the two holds that separated the prisoners and caused ceiling beams and planking to come crashing down on the men below. A couple hundred of the POWs were killed, most in the forward hold, and another 200 were injured. Most of the medical staff was in the forward hold, which received the most damage and had the most casualties. Although George and Max were in the forward hold, they were among the fortunate few who managed to survive the blasts without major injuries. One survivor described it as looking like a human butcher shop.

The bomb blasts created smoke and confusion and caused George and Max to initially become separated. They frantically searched for each other through the debris and the dead and injured men, but the smoke made it difficult to breathe as well as to see. Finally, after finding each other safe and without serious injury, they began helping the injured men around them.

Many of the POWs were so badly injured from the bomb blasts that they were unrecognizable. Several of the men went into shock and others were screaming in pain from their injuries. With the loss of so many medical staff it was difficult for many of the injured men to receive the medical attention they needed. Additionally, without proper medical supplies, the remaining medical staff was greatly limited as to what they could do for the injured men. They mostly prepared bandages from whatever scraps of clothing the men would volunteer or they could pull off the dead. The next day, on January 10th, a small group of Japanese medics came on board and provided some dressing to those not seriously wounded. They would not even bother with the more seriously injured,

Brothers Born of Adversity

who they expected to die. However, they did leave some bandages and medicine with the POW medical staff. At this point, nearly half of the original count of 1,619 prisoners who had begun the voyage on the *Oryoku Maru* were dead.

The bodies of the dead were stacked in piles near the hatch doors. For two days the prisoners were not allowed to bury their dead, whose bodies had now become bloated. The smell was horrific. On January 12th they were finally given permission to remove the dead and volunteers were requested to help in this effort. This would have been a difficult task for healthy men, let alone men who were weak and exhausted. By this time, most of the men had lost about 40 pounds of body weight. About 30 men, many of whom were corpsmen, volunteered to remove the 350 dead POWs on board. Since the ship was in a harbor, the dead could not be buried at sea as they had previously done on the voyage. For the volunteers it meant the possibility to get some water to drink. As corpsmen, it is likely that George and Max would have been involved in assisting with this effort. The dead bodies of the POWs were hoisted by rope either individually or by cargo sling from the ship and on to small boats or barges called sampans. The sampans were poled through the water by Formosan civilians. Prior to the removal of the dead, it was said that some POWs could be seen sitting on dead bodies while eating their meager rations in the crowded conditions. The prisoners who were still alive had become numb to the conditions around them - it was now primarily just about trying to survive.

For two days sampans hauled the bodies to a point near the beach where large piles of coal were kept. From that point the volunteers would remove the bodies from the sampans and drag the bodies to shore. The bodies were then loaded on wagons and transported to an area near the beach where they were buried in a mass grave. The following year a team of American soldiers dug up the remains and had them reburied at the National Memorial Cemetery in Hawaii. Since the remains were mingled together and could not be identified by individual, they were all interred among 20 mass graves with each grave marked as Unknown.

On January 13, 1945, the POWs were advised that all of them would now be transferred to the holds on the *Brazil Maru* since the *Enoura Maru* had been too badly damaged to continue the voyage. George, Max, and the remaining men who made the trip from the Philippines to Formosa on the *Brazil Maru*, now found themselves back aboard that ship. However, the conditions were much more crowded than before. The *Brazil Maru* had also been badly damaged from earlier bombing but had quickly been repaired. Because of the extent of these damages some of the men thought they must be on a different ship. Transfer of the prisoners to the *Brazil Maru* was again done using the sampans. Many of the men had injuries or fractures and had to be hoisted out of the hold and onto the sampans, which was a difficult and painful process for them. One POW who had both his legs and arms injured managed to drag himself along the deck to ensure he would not be left behind. Some men went into shock from the pain, while others died in the process. By the evening of January 13th with all the remaining POWs transferred to the *Brazil Maru*, it left the harbor with a convoy of other ships. This was the remaining leg of the voyage to Japan for the POWs. Despite the enormity of the suffering that George, Max, and their fellow prisoners had endured, this next leg of their trip may well have been the worst.

The trip from Takao, Formosa to Moji, Japan took 17 horrific days, from January 13th to the 29th, to complete. There were two primary reasons the voyage took so long; first, the ship was skirting the Chinese coast in hopes of avoiding American submarines and planes; and second, the *Brazil Maru* had changed course to rescue and tow other damaged Japanese ships to port. For the first two days back out at sea, the POWs were given nothing to drink, lived in crowded filthy conditions, and suffered with diarrhea, dysentery, and pneumonia as well. Now, instead of contending with the tropical heat, they were experiencing frigid temperatures. Having the hatch door open allowed the men to get fresh air and light, but it also allowed in the cold, rain, and snow. The prisoners begged Mr. Wada and the guards for relief but were generally ignored. Fewer than half the men had straw mats to lie on to keep them off the steel flooring. To make things even worse, in one of the holds a ventilator blew frigid air on the men. The Japanese refused to repair it.

The first night out from Takao, 15 POWs died, and the number grew to as many as 40 in a single night before reaching Moji, Japan. George and Max and the other corpsmen played a key role in helping break up fights, distribute food, and tend to the needs of the sick and dying. They would also strip the clothing from the bodies of the dead and redistribute it to the living. The bodies of the dead would be accumulated over a two or three-day period before they were allowed to be brought up to the deck and thrown overboard. As on the earlier voyages, the Japanese did not allow any religious services for the dead. It was now just an emotionless process that they had to perform. While there were certainly diseases among the men, the primary reasons for the high death count continued to be malnutrition, exposure to the elements, and dehydration. Only a quarter cup of rice was provided for each prisoner per day. Since the medical staff, including corpsmen, were the only prisoners still working as they cared for the other prisoners, it was agreed that they would be given a somewhat larger portion of rice.

Madness continued to plague the prisoners as many would reach their breaking point. For some, death seemed like a more viable option than the suffering they were in. As they made their rounds, the corpsmen routinely shouted to bay leaders to *"roll out your dead."* Often the dead had already been stripped naked. In George Weller's book, *First into Nagasaki*, he states that, *"The corpsmen who worked all night were perhaps the most unqualifiedly admired of the hardworking medicos."* He then quoted Max as saying, *"You not only had to hustle those buckets for the men on the hatch, but you also had to stop fights in the bays for the clothing of others who had gone."* In Manny Lawton's book, *Some Survived*, he also commented that *"Medical corpsmen on duty showed a nobleness of character and a resolution of purpose which was uncommon, considering that they themselves were weak and hungry. It was their duty to nurse the sick, comfort the wounded and gather the dead. Never did I see them act with impatience or callousness in ministering to their charges. Among those who worked diligently were Frank L. Maxwell of Birmingham; Dean A. Coburn, Charleston; Estel Myers, Louisville; John T. Istock, Pittsburg; and Oscar Otero of Los Lunas, New Mexico."*

Among the POWs were several military chaplains who offered evening prayers and did their best to console the men until they too had been overburdened trying to take care of the men. It was said that one chaplain gave his food and water to a man he was caring for even though it hastened his own death. In another instance a chaplain stood for long hours to allow men a little more room to lie. However, like the rest of the men, the chaplains were not immune from the pain, death, and derangement that afflicted so many of them. Only two or three of approximately a dozen chaplains who started the voyage on the *Oryoku Maru* survived the trip to Japan. Often, while they were able, they could be heard consoling the men and leading them in prayer. It was not uncommon to hear them reciting the 23rd Psalm to someone they were consoling:

> *"The Lord is my shepherd; I shall not want.*
> *He makes me to lie down in green pastures;*
> *He leads me beside the still waters. He restores my soul;*
> *He leads me in the paths of righteousness for His name's sake.*
> *Yea, though I walk through the valley of the shadow of death,*
> *I will fear no evil; For You are with me;*
> *Your rod and Your staff, they comfort me.*
> *You prepare a table before me in the presence of my enemies;*
> *You anoint my head with oil; My cup runs over.*
> *Surely goodness and mercy shall follow me*
> *All the days of my life;*
> *And I will dwell in the house of the Lord forever."*

Among the chaplains was a Catholic army lieutenant named Father William "Bill" Cummings, who, in a sermon on Bataan, had been the first one to use the phrase, "There are no atheists in foxholes." This catchphrase would become a well-known saying, particularly among Christians. It was observed that the men were much more attentive and respectful to the chaplains' prayers whenever the ships were under aerial attack. Father Cummings' services each day were an expected part of the daily routine until he too became too weak and subsequently died.

In G. Kurt Piehler's book, *A Religious History of the American GI in World War II*, he notes that, "*Despite the protected status of chaplains under the Geneva Convention as clergy and officers, chaplains died at a greater rate than other GIs.*" He also noted that, "*The experiences of army and naval chaplains held in captivity reads like a life of modern-day martyrs. Many strived to continue to hold religious services, conduct Bible studies, counsel prisoners, and bury the dead.*" Despite the important

Brothers Born of Adversity

contribution chaplains made during World War II, their roles were often overlooked in books and movies relating to the war.

Mr. Wada had given the men strict orders not to touch the bags of sugar in the hold or they would face severe repercussions; however, at this point it didn't really seem to matter to the men. Of course, eating the raw sugar in the men's weakened condition also created its own problems with the men's digestive systems. An additional benefit of consuming the sugar was that it was stored in bags that could be used as mats and covering. After finding that the POWs had been helping themselves to some of the sugar, Mr. Wada threatened to cut off all water and rice to both holds unless those who had been stealing the sugar were turned over to the guards for appropriate punishment. To keep all the men from being punished, Lt. Colonel Beecher asked for two volunteers who would offer themselves as sacrifices to save the lives of their fellow POWs. He promised that whoever volunteered, if they survived whatever the Japanese did to them, he would see to it that they were taken care of and wouldn't have to go without food the rest of the trip. A husky English sergeant named Trapp, who did not go ashore with the other Britons at Formosa, and a burly sergeant named Arda "Max" Hanenkrat, who was a medical aidman of the 31st Infantry, volunteered. By volunteering, these two brave men agreed to offer themselves to the Japanese and to take whatever punishment that would befall them, which could mean their death. Above deck, the two men were beaten unconscious, revived, and then beaten again as their fellow POWs listened for the sound of gunfire, an indication that the men had been shot. After some time, the Japanese pushed the badly beaten men back into the hold. While the two incredibly brave volunteers were, for the moment spared their lives, they would both ultimately die from the abuse they had endured before they reached the shores of Japan.

Throughout the journey there continued to be some active trading between the guards and the POWs. At this point, officers were willing to part with their most treasured possessions, such as their wedding rings and Annapolis or West Point rings. In exchange, they could obtain some food, water, or cigarettes. This, of course, brought resentment on the part of the enlisted men who had nothing left to trade. Ted Lewin, who could speak some Japanese and was on the food and work detail, used

Brothers Born of Adversity

his skills in negotiating and bribing to persuade the cook to add a little extra food or trade something with a guard for a little extra water. If any were caught, whether guard or POW, they could expect to be punished. In Ted Lewin's deposition at the war crimes trial after the war, he recalled a protestant chaplain named Brown who came to him with a small gold object containing jade in its middle. The chaplain asked him if he would trade it with the guards for some water. He managed to trade it for one canteen cup of tea. However, despite drinking the tea, the chaplain died the following day.

A couple of times a day, roll call would still be performed and if a prisoner had died someone would say *"dead"* and maybe provide the reason. Some reported that Lewin and his associates kept some of the dead propped up as if they were still alive so that they could get their share of rations. The men shivered from the cold and huddled close together for warmth. In the corner of one of the bays some of the men found a few old ragged and dirty life preservers. Those who found the life preservers immediately began tearing them apart and stuffing the matting into their shirts and pants to provide a little warmth from the frigid temperatures. However, they soon realized the life preservers were full of lice and they would not be able to stop scratching throughout the rest of the voyage.

Throughout the voyage the men agonized in thirst. Since sufficient water should have been available after stopping in Formosa, the men felt that the Japanese were deliberately trying to kill them. Men would attempt to catch drops of rain or flakes of snow that fell through the hatch opening. With so many dying, it seemed that death no longer meant anything -- if you died, you died. One POW was said to have struck himself on the head with his canteen in an effort to kill himself and was, surprisingly, successful. Even Commander Bridget, who had been a tower of strength and leadership, succumbed to sickness and died. As men continued to die, they would be hoisted up to the deck with a rope around their ankles and then shoved overboard into the water.

A private named William Surber, who was near death, crawled over to two surviving chaplains in hopes of being baptized before his death. The chaplains were too weak to understand what he wanted. A friend, Chief

Brothers Born of Adversity

Yeoman Theodore Brownell, called the private back and said he would baptize him. Not having any water, he used some saliva from his parched mouth and dampened his finger, which he then placed on the private's forehead as he had seen in church or had watched the chaplains do. He then baptized the private in the name of the Father, Son, and Holy Spirit. The newly baptized private then laid down to sleep in peace, not to awaken again in any earthly surroundings.

Mr. Wada continued to show little concern with all the men dying but would habitually ask Lt. Colonel Beecher for a roster of the living. Finally, Lt. Colonel Beecher told him *"Never mind the roster - no need for a roster - everybody would be dead."* Mr. Wada gave no response.

Brothers Born of Adversity

Chapter 8 – Arriving in Japan and Fukuoka POW Camp #17

Finally, on January 29, 1945, the *Brazil Maru* arrived in Moji, Japan. The port city of Moji is on the northern end of the island of Kyushu, which is the southern-most of the larger island chain that makes up Japan. At the time, manufacturing and the mining of coal and other natural resources were performed on the island. About mid-way down the island on the western side was the industrial city of Nagasaki.

Upon their arrival in Moji, it was estimated that only 425 to 435 POWs or about 25 percent of the original 1,619 who left Manila December 13, 1944, on the *Oryoku Maru*, were still alive. Yet, over the next several weeks, dozens more of these survivors would die as well.

At the docks, a group of Japanese officers and personnel met and boarded the *Brazil Maru* upon its arrival. The Japanese officers summoned the senior officer among the POWs, Lt. Colonel Beecher, who was now nearly too weak and exhausted to stand before them. Although the Japanese officers tried not to show it, it was obvious that they were shocked by the condition of the men. By this time the men were walking skeletons, filthy and lice infested, with matted beards and wearing inadequate clothing for such frigid weather conditions. Max was quoted by a reporter upon liberation that he had weighed 172 pounds when he had left Bilibid, but only weighed 94 pounds by the time he reached Japan. Most likely this was a misquote; the reporter meant Max weighed 172 pounds when he first entered Bilibid. In any event, Max had lost significant weight during his imprisonment. George's military records indicated that he had lost 50 pounds during his time as a POW.

When the Japanese officers climbed down in the hold they were overcome by the smell of urine, excrement, and the sight of 52 bodies of dead POWs stacked in a pile. The POWs were ordered to climb out of the holds and to line up on deck. Many of the men had to be assisted out of the hold by their fellow POWs. They were then ordered to remove whatever clothes they had on despite it being a bitterly cold day with many sick from pneumonia. The men were then sprayed with a disinfectant and some fresh clothes were distributed, although not

Brothers Born of Adversity

enough for all the men. Japanese doctors who examined the men realized that many of them had dysentery and that all of them would need to be tested by running a tube up their rectums. Some of the corpsmen thought it strange that the Japanese decided to test the dead as well. One young brave navy officer named Barton Cross, breathed his last breath while lying there on the deck.

The men were directed to get off the ship and onto the dock and then to walk about two blocks to a factory warehouse. Volunteers were requested to help take some of the most ill men to waiting ambulances for transport to a hospital. In their weakened condition the men could barely shuffle along while others needed to be supported by their fellow POWs. Some were carried to the warehouse by compassionate Japanese dock workers who volunteered to help. Again, Japanese guards would try to hurry the men along, shouting "*speedo, speedo*!." They would beat those who fell until they were back on their feet or their fellow POWs could help them back up. Some of the Japanese children would spit on the men as they walked pass. Many of the adults along the way could be seen putting handkerchiefs to their faces, repulsed by the smell and appearance of the passing prisoners.

Once the POWs arrived at the unheated warehouse they were provided with some blankets and raincoats to protect them from the cold. There was also fresh clean water to drink from barrels that had frozen over. Roll call was taken again and an interpreter spoke to them about many things; one of which was the importance of not wasting food, as if that were likely to be a problem with these nearly starved men. Finally, the men were provided a meal of clean white rice with some radishes in it, which seemed like a banquet to the men. They were then allowed to bathe and given some additional clothes. One survivor later recalled how he soiled his clean new pants shortly after putting them on from an attack of diarrhea; a fate that may have happened to several of the POWs. This was very likely the reason some of those entering the POW camps were described as being nearly naked when they arrived. The remaining POWs were then divided up into three groups and sent to various POW camps in the Fukuoka district, which covered most of the north and central area of the island of Kyushu.

Brothers Born of Adversity

From the warehouse, the men were forced to walk to the train station and loaded into train cars with wooden benches and toilet facilities in each car. Guards were posted at each of the entrances to the cars. The window blinds were pulled so that the men couldn't see out. Whenever a man had an opportunity to peek out through the blinds, he could often see vast amounts of devastation that the Allied bombers had inflicted on the country.

The first group of POWs to be taken from the train was primarily made up of officers who were assigned to Camp #3, where some American POWs were already being housed. This camp was about an hour's train ride out of Moji. The next group of men was taken to Camp #1, also known as the Pine Tree Camp. This camp was about five hours out of Moji at the city of Kashii. It would be several more hours before George, Max, and the rest of those assigned to Camp #17 would reach their destination, despite it being only about 90 miles south of Moji. Camp #17 was located at the city of Omuta and had been built on reclaimed land along the bay or the Ariake Sea as it was called. About 40 miles to the southwest, on a peninsula across the bay, was the city of Nagasaki.

The exact number of POWs sent by ambulance to the hospital, those assigned to one of the three camps, and those who died shortly thereafter vary by source. In George Weller's book *First into Nagasaki*, he provides the following breakdown of where and how many of these surviving POWs were placed and the estimated number who died at each location. According to his estimates, only about 274 POWs, or about 17 percent, of the initial 1,619 POWs shipped out on the *Oryoku Maru* actually survived to see liberation. However, again these estimates vary by source. Additionally, there is not a good accounting of the number of British and Dutch POWs disembarked at Formosa who survived the war. Below are the estimates provided by George Weller:
-   Of the approximately 135 survivors taken to the hospital in Moji, about 85 would eventually die there.
-   Of the approximately 100, mostly officers, taken to Camp #3, about 31 would later die there.
-   Of the approximately 100 officers taken to Camp #1, about 30 would later die there.

Brothers Born of Adversity

- Of the 97 prisoners taken to Camp #17, 15 would later die there. (It was this group that George, Max, and Ted Lewin were part of. Other sources say that the number of men who died in this group was more like 24.)

In the book, *No Time for Geishas*, the author Geoffrey Pharaoh Adams, writes about the arrival of the group of POWs at Camp #17. He stated, *"They arrived in open trucks on a bitter cold day, some naked, none with more than a single cotton blanket to protect them from the cutting wind. We put them into a hut which had been specifically emptied for them; and during the next few weeks they died, two some days, three another."* He also added, *"Of all that wretched company, one man alone stood out – well clothed, well-fed, and bitterly hated. His name was Lewin..."*

George Weller, in *First into Nagasaki*, also makes mention of their arrival. When upon seeing the men, the American camp medical doctor was asked how many of them had died. His response was, *"If you want to see dead men, there they stand before you."* The POWs who survived the hellish voyage would have needed days or weeks to recover from their ordeal before they could be put to work. As noted earlier, anywhere from 15 to 24 of the POWs died after their arrival in the camp. Upon their arrival, George was still recovering from his shrapnel wounds, as well as suffering from severe undernourishment. Max had developed pneumonia and was sick for two months. He considered himself lucky, since somehow the American doctors managed to get some sulfadiazine for him and he was able to pull through. George may have had a hand in obtaining this medicine for Max, since his son, Perry, recalled his father mentioning that he helped get some needed medicine for Max during their captivity.

The city of Omuta was home to the Mitsui Coal Mining Company owned by the Baron Mitsui, a member of a group of families that controlled much of the industry in Japan. The Fukuoka Camp #17 was the largest of the prison camps in the region and contained close to 2,000 British, Australian, Dutch, and American POWs who were used to supplement the labor force in the coal mining operation and the production of zinc. The camp contained 33 one story barracks surrounded by a high wooden and wire fence. Each of the wooden

Brothers Born of Adversity

barracks was about 120' x 16' with tar paper roofs and was generally divided into about 10 rooms or cubicles. The rooms were furnished with wooden beds and straw mats for the prisoners. The rooms had windows with glass or paper panes. Each room also had one 15-watt light bulb which was controlled by the guards and not turned out at night. The barracks were not heated during the winter months and insufficient blankets were provided to keep the men warm in their malnourished condition. The officers among the POWs would be placed about three or four to a room and enlisted men about four to six. The camp had originally been used by laborers working for the Mitsui Coal Mining Company. But with the start of the war, it had been expanded and in 1943 converted to a prison camp for POWs who were being used as laborers in the mines or zinc foundry. The mining company leased the prisoners from the military, and in turn the military would pay the prisoners 15 yen a day. This was less than a penny a day at the time. Officers would be paid somewhat more than the enlistees. Although both George and Max were corpsmen, they were needed more to work as laborers in the coal mines. Max was allowed to work in the pharmacy for about a month while he was still recovering, but then was put to work in the coal mines as well. While George and Max were recovering after their arrival in Japan, the prison camps around Manila were being liberated by General MacArthur and Allied troops.

Overall view of Camp #17 Omuta, Japan. Public domain photo courtesy of *WWII Japanese POW Camp Fukuoka #17* website maintained by Linda Dahl Weeks.

Brothers Born of Adversity

Outside each of the prison rooms a board was affixed that contained rows of nails by each of the occupant's assigned number. The different nails under each number represented different locations where a prisoner might be, i.e., work, mess hall, toilet, bath house, etc. Whenever a man would leave or return to his room, he was required to place the wooden tag he was assigned to the proper nail. All too often men would forget to move their tag when dashing off to the toilet or returning exhausted from work. If a guard found a tag on the wrong nail, he would carry it to the guard room and the offending prisoner would have to reclaim his tag from the guards. The prisoner could expect to be interrogated over it, have his face slapped, and in some cases receive a brutal beating.

Toilets were located at the end of each of the barracks and consisted of hollow stools over concrete tanks that needed to be emptied twice a week. Cold water faucets were available outside and between the barracks along with wooden wash tubs where the men could hand wash their clothes. Nearby, there were clothes lines where they could hang their clothes to dry, but if one didn't keep a careful watch on their clothes they would often be stolen. The camp bathing facility was in a separate building and contained two heated tubs in Japanese style, which were approximately 30 feet long, 10 feet wide, and four feet deep and could accommodate around 75 men at a time. The American officer in charge prohibited the men from going into the pools during the summer for fear of catching or spreading skin diseases. In the winter months the men were permitted to go in the tubs only after rinsing off first, but there was still a concern that men could pass out from the heat in their weakened condition and drown if they weren't properly watched.

Brothers Born of Adversity

Camp bath tubs. 75-man capacity. Public domain photo courtesy of *WWII Japanese POW Camp Fukuoka #17* website maintained by Linda Dahl Weeks.

At the camp, a Lieutenant Little ran the mess hall under the direction of a Japanese mess sergeant. They were assisted by about 15 POWs, some of whom had been professional cooks. The menu generally consisted of steamed rice and a vegetable soup that provided very little protein. Occasionally the Japanese would bring in dog meat to include in the soup, which was difficult for some of the men to eat even with their near starvation diet. Men working in the mines would be given buns to eat on their break. The average POW lost about 60 pounds during his imprisonment. Red Cross packages containing food and medicine were given out very sparingly to the prisoners while the Japanese officers helped themselves to what they wanted.

Elaborate theatrics were performed when Red Cross inspections were scheduled to take place. Food and medicine supplies would be set out for the prisoners as if it was normal. The sick would be removed from the medical camp hospital to another building and replaced by some of the healthiest looking men. Female nurses would be brought in from a local hospital and act as if they were providing care for the patients in the hospital. Prisoners knew that if they said anything to the inspectors that there would be severe repercussions once the inspectors left. As soon as the inspectors left, the food and medicine that had been placed around would quickly be removed, the nurses returned to the hospital in town,

Brothers Born of Adversity

the sick men returned to the hospital, and the healthy men returned to the mines or wherever they had been assigned.

Fortunately, the prison camp did have a medical facility that had some surgical equipment and accommodations for about 30 patients. While the facility was under the direction of a Japanese doctor, it was generally staffed by medical staff among the POWs, including a couple of American doctors, a dentist, and some of the corpsmen. Medical supplies were very limited. The American doctors in the camp were generally young and not well experienced but had been quickly gaining their medical skills treating the wide array of injuries and illnesses that were common in the camp. Most of the illnesses in the camp were related to poor nutrition, as well as diseases such as pneumonia, tuberculosis, malaria, skin diseases, and something the doctors simply called "Fukuoka Fever."

Surgeries were conducted in the camp with limited medical supplies and anesthesia. Rubber gloves were not available, so surgeries were conducted with bare hands. Generally, injuries were the result of mining accidents or beatings.

Regarding the psychological and social problems of the prisoners, Dr. Hewlett, a surviving POW of Camp #17, had later written that *"The philosophy of the prisoners of war is a strange one, individually developed to make survival possible in the most hostile environment. He first learned to laugh at the tragedies that comprised the everyday life. He completely obliterated the pangs of hunger. The starving man would willingly trade his meager ration for a few cigarettes. In many instances he would risk his rations gambling with professionals who pursued their trade without compassion for any life except their own."*

The coal mines that many of the men worked in had nearly been exhausted of coal, but the Japanese were attempting to extract every bit of usable coal they could. The mines were deep and actually ran under the bay. Wood timbers in the mines were being pulled out so that coal on the ceiling of the tunnels could be removed, making conditions in the mines very dangerous. Before entering the mines, the prisoners were required to bow to a Buddhist Shrine, which for Christians and Jews would have been considered blasphemy. However, officers convinced the men that they could say their prayers to the Christian/Judeo God quietly to themselves, as they bowed, and therefore, they would not be guilty of worshipping idols. This helped to mitigate another potential conflict with the guards. The men worked on a 10-day work schedule. As a result, they had every 10th day off to do laundry and such, as well as have some time for rest and relaxation. Although the Geneva Convention secured the right of freedom of religion and the right of POWs to attend services of their own faith, they were not allowed any religious services while imprisoned in the camp.

Discipline in the camp was strict. Failure to follow camp regulations precisely could result in a face slapping, a painful beating, or worse. One had to properly march, Japanese style, while keeping one's hands straight. POWs also had to learn to properly bow and learn to respond appropriately to the Japanese commands. For someone like George, who always seemed to have a bit of a problem with authority, being imprisoned under such circumstances was particularly challenging and resulted in his share of beatings and getting his face slapped. Max, on the other hand, was much better at not reacting or showing his contempt for his captors and would often try to coach George into letting an offense go to avoid punishment.

Many of the camp survivors interviewed by the reporter and writer, George Weller, recalled the brutal beatings that they endured during their imprisonment. Some were tortured with electrical current while some were forced to kneel on sticks of bamboo for hours. In one such instance, two POWs were beaten badly and thrown down in the snow. Sharp pieces of wood or bamboo were placed behind their knees while they kneeled. Then the Japanese guards would ride their backs, while the men screamed in pain. They were forced to do this so long that one of the men developed gangrene in both his legs and had to have them amputated. After healing from the ordeal, the man with the amputated legs would be carried around the camp on the back of his friend. Such adversity created incredible bonds of loyalty among many of the men. Some of the guards solicited sexual favors from the POWs in exchange for a little food and cigarettes. In other instances, a prisoner might have no choice. Some of the overseers in the mines would amuse themselves by beating a man at random each lunchtime. Others reported a water

Brothers Born of Adversity

punishment where a man's hands would be tied behind his back and then he was forced to lie on his back with his mouth open while guards poured him full of as much water as possible. Afterwards, the guards would jump on his stomach until he was dead. Such abuses were truly hellish.

One of their favorite winter punishments was to throw cold water on the offending POW and then place him in an unheated cell for days. In one reported incident a young private was caught by the Japanese taking a Red Cross parcel. These parcels were supposed to be for the prisoners but had not been issued to them. As punishment, the Camp Commandant had the private tied to a post and ordered that his men use him as bayonet practice. In another incident, a man who was a lay preacher was caught talking to one of the Korean workers in the mine, presumably sharing his Christian faith. He was severely beaten and murdered for the offense. After the war, the Camp's Japanese Commandant was tried by the Allied forces for war crimes and hanged.

Of course, not all the Japanese soldiers were monsters. Sometimes an officer might stop a beating or overlook a small infraction, but these incidents seemed few and far between. What seemed strange to the POWs was that after a prisoner died, the Japanese would conduct a fairly elaborate funeral of sorts for the deceased man. Some of the man's ashes from his cremation would be placed in a jar and retained in a room in one of the barracks as if to honor the dead.

Several sources mention that Camp #17 had the reputation of being the roughest among the Fukuoka prison camps. Geoffrey Adams' book, *No Time for Geishas*, elaborates as to why it had this reputation. Adams had been a British officer imprisoned at Camp #17 from June 1944 to April 1945. According to Adams, there was a noticeable contrast between the prisoners' appearances. He noticed that some of the men looked better dressed and nourished than others, and it soon became obvious to him why. In contrast to the many good and honorable men in the camp, he writes that there was a group of Americans who referred to themselves as the "Democrats," while others referred to them as the "American Mafia." To be clear, there is no indication that this group had any formal affiliation with the political party of the same name, but this was what they called themselves. As for those who were not part of their group, the Democrats referred to them as Republicans. Adams does not name the ringleader of this group by his actual name, but it is clear that he was referring to Lt. Little, the mess hall officer. Lt. Little and two of his comrades each had their own rooms in the galley area where they lived. According to Adams, these men had ingratiated themselves to the Japanese and were willing to sacrifice their own comrades if it were to their advantage. He considered them a separate enemy element in the camp for which they always had to be on their guard. With the arrival of Ted Lewin, Adams commented that Lewin would find himself among his *"fellow-spirits."*

With its limited availability, food became a form of currency in the camp. According to Adams, the "Democrats," always looking for an opportunity, began a form of loansharking, offering some extra rice today to be repaid in a couple days with interest in the form of a cup of soup. Failure to pay usually resulted in being beaten up in some dark corner, and interest in the form of food provisions continued to accrue. Food illicitly obtained by this group was used to buy cigarettes, personal items, and even sexual favors. The theft or trading of food had become blatant. It is said that Lt. Little tried to put a stop to it, at least among those who were not part of his group. He reported a corporal to their Japanese captors even though that meant a brutal death for the corporal. The corporal received several beatings before being starved to death over a 39 day-period. Adams provides much more detail of the abuse by this group, but for the purpose of this story, sufficient information has already been provided to give the reader a glimpse of the horrors that the POWs experienced in Fukuoka Camp #17.

After the war, many of the POWs filed complaints against Lt. Little, who was subsequently court-martialed. However, after a five-month trial he was found not guilty and allowed to finish out his military career.

While the mood in the camp was depressing and full of despair, it didn't keep the men from their habit of giving nicknames to their Japanese captors. These included, Brown Bomber, Flangeface, Sugar Lips, Shitbird, Pig, Screamer, Riverside, Squeaky, Clark Gable, Sailor, Devil, Mule, Donald Duck, Tom Mix, etc. If caught showing any disrespect to their captors their punishment would be severe. Nicknames were not just

Brothers Born of Adversity

used for their captors. One American doctor in the prison camp had been nicknamed "Rigor Mortis," and another officer was affectionately nicknamed "Mother." Some of the diseases in the camps were also given nicknames, such as "Hirohito's Curse" and "Benjo Boogie." Sometimes prisoners working in the mine would injure themselves to get out of work and away from some of the brutish guards. One POW assigned to work in the mines had considered himself a failed amateur actor prior to the war. By putting a little bit of soap in his mouth and working up a mouthful of froth, he put on his greatest acting performance, convincing the guards and even the American doctors that he had lost his mind. After being assigned a much better job working in the camp garden, he seemed to gradually regain his senses.

Several weeks after George and Max's arrival at Camp #17, yet another threat emerged. American bombers were now routinely flying overhead and destroying targets in the Omuta area. The Japanese placed anti-aircraft crews and weapons in the corners of the prison camp, which would make the camp a more attractive target to the U.S. military. Some believed that this may have been a deliberate attempt to get the camp bombed and eliminate the prisoners. During one night attack the camp was in fact bombed, setting ablaze the camp hospital along with some of the barracks. The city of Omuta was also greatly damaged and many of the POWs were loaded onto trucks and taken into the city to help bury the dead. On at least one occasion, prisoners were required to dig out unexploded bombs that had landed in the soft mud along the bay near the camp. The Japanese had the POWs build bomb shelters which were essentially long trenches with about three feet of waste from the mines placed over the top. Whenever planes were heard or spotted, the Japanese would herd the POWs into these shelters. With all of this activity the POWs thought surely the end of the war was near. However, credible rumors circulated that, if Allied forces landed on the island, all Allied prisoners would be killed. At this point there were approximately 140,000 POWs serving as laborers in Japan.

Brothers Born of Adversity

Yard outside barracks. Notice trees leaning to the left, the result of bomb concussion. Public domain photo courtesy of *WWII Japanese POW Camp Fukuoka #17* website maintained by Linda Dahl Weeks.

The POWs were forbidden to read any newspapers or discuss the war effort. Japanese newspapers were still predicting a Japanese victory and made claims that Japan had bombed London and was attacking New York City. In reality, Germany had surrendered on May 7, 1945, and the Allied forces were closing in on Japan with a huge invasion force. By early 1945, the Allies had been steadily conquering Japanese held islands in the Pacific and moving closer toward the Japanese main islands. Of strategic importance to the Allies in preparing for the eventual invasion of Japan were the Okinawa Islands which were 340 miles south of the main Japanese Islands.

Brothers Born of Adversity

Chapter 9 – George's Sisters Enter the Combat Zone

While George and Max were languishing in the prison camp, George's sisters Thelma and Aller Crowell, who had been serving as army nurses in the Caribbean, volunteered for duty in the Pacific. They had hopes of being closer to their brother and finding him once he was released from his prison camp. A younger sister, Gene Crowell, completed her nursing training during the war and began serving as an army nurse in Europe. On March 29, 1945, Thelma and Aller departed Fort Lawton in Seattle, Washington, and traveled by ship, making a stop in Oahu, Hawaii. From there they continued across the Pacific to the coast of Okinawa, arriving on April 16, 1945. Not being accustomed to traveling by ship, they were both sick for most of the voyage, as well as overwhelmed by the heat.

The battle for the main island of Okinawa, a Japanese possession, began on April 1, 1945. The battle lasted for over 80 days and was one of the bloodiest of the war. Female nurses were not allowed to go on shore for the first month or so but worked on hospital ships off the coast of Okinawa. However, this would prove to be equally or more dangerous as hundreds of Kamikaze aircraft attacked and destroyed Allied ships for the first two months of the battle, including two hospital ships.

Photo of sisters Aller and Thelma Crowell. Photo from family's collection.

Brothers Born of Adversity

By early June 1945, Aller came ashore with the 68th Field hospital as Chief Nurse and her sister Thelma was detached from the 75th Station hospital and given orders to serve with her on June 8, 1945. The monsoon rains had begun, making military and medical operations all the more difficult. Thelma later recalled that there was no time to set up the larger Station hospital to which she was assigned as the casualties were heavy and all the doctors had to pitch in and work in the field hospitals. The 68th was located on the eastern side of the island near the southern end of Okinawa. The Field hospital consisted of tents situated in a low valley where soon the ground was soaked by the monsoon rains and became just fields and hills of mud. Medical transport vehicles were often mired in the mud. Decaying and swollen bodies of unburied Japanese and American soldiers, teeming with maggots, filled the air with the smell of death.

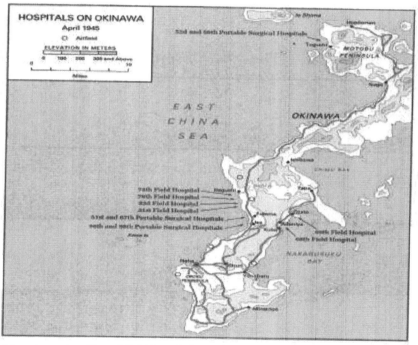

Map shows location of field hospitals on the Island of Okinawa. The Japanese had dug in their defenses on the south side of the island from Naha on the west to Yonabaru on the east coast. Map from U.S. Army publication, *The Medical Department: Medical Service in the War Against Japan.*

Brothers Born of Adversity

Young soldiers, who the sisters referred to as the "boys," were assigned to guard the 68th. They used tripwire flares to detect any Japanese soldiers trying to infiltrate the hospital. The guards were deployed in individual foxhole positions behind the wire encircling the entire camp. This deployment within the jungle prevented them from talking to one another during the night. This also made many of them anxious and more than a little scared.

At times, a tripwire flare would go off and the soldiers would start shooting in the general direction of the disturbance. This alerted the other guards and they would start shooting as well. Soon bullets were going in all directions, including toward the tents where the nurses were sleeping. Thelma and Aller would later recall how everyone would roll off their cots and hit the deck whenever this occurred. Fortunately, they did not recall any American casualties from these incidents. Finally, someone in charge would give the cease fire order, or in some cases the guards would just run out of ammo and the shooting would stop. Thelma and Aller did recall that on occasion, the "boys" would actually shoot a Japanese soldier during the night. This was for them a small victory and cause for celebration. The "boys" would string up the dead, bullet-riddled body of the Japanese soldier right in front of the mess hall of the hospital. The sisters recalled that it didn't affect their appetite and they simply felt glad that another Japanese soldier was dead.

Sometime after the fighting on the island had ended with the capture of Okinawa, Thelma and Aller would move with the 68th Field hospital to Korea where Aller would remain the chief nurse until the unit was deactivated.

The role and scope that military nurses like Thelma and Aller engaged in during World War II should not be overlooked. It has been estimated that there were roughly 8,700 army and navy nurses in the U.S. military before the war. After the surprise attack on Pearl Harbor, a major national recruiting campaign began to increase the number of nurses available to serve. By the end of the war, there were over 70,000 nurses in the military. The skill and determination of military nurses contributed to a high survival rate among post-injury American soldiers who were fortunate enough to receive their care. As a direct result of their service,

Brothers Born of Adversity

over 460 nurses lost their lives during the war. Among the Allied forces on Bataan and Corregidor that surrendered were 77 female nurses who would be held as POWs in the Philippines until the islands were liberated. These nurses were known as the "Angels of Bataan and Corregidor."

Photo from U.S. National Library of Medicine. Taken in June 1945 of the 76th Field Hospital, shows what conditions would have been like in field hospitals on Okinawa at the time.

Brothers Born of Adversity

Chapter 10 – The Atomic Bomb and Liberation

Unbeknownst to all but a select group, the United States had developed a secret atomic weapon that would forever change the potential destructiveness of such a great war. President Franklin Roosevelt had died on April 12, 1945, and his Vice President, Harry Truman, had become President. In weighing the cost of the potential number of American lives that would be lost in a land invasion, President Truman made the difficult decision to use this new atomic weapon in an effort to bring the war to a close. As a result, after nearly four years of war, on August 6, 1945, the United States dropped an atomic bomb nicknamed "Little Boy" on the city of Hiroshima. It has been estimated that about 100,000 Japanese men, women, and children died as a result of the explosion and the resulting radiation. Three days later, on August 9, 1945, the United States dropped the second atomic bomb, this one named "Fat Man," on the city of Nagasaki, killing an estimated 40,000 more people.

Hiroshima was located about 180 miles northeast of Omuta and Camp #17 while Nagasaki lay about 40 miles away to the southwest. Many of the POWs in Camp #17 witnessed the mushroom cloud rising over Nagasaki, although they did not realize what it was at the time. One man said it transformed from a red ball suspended in the air to a mushroom cloud rising up like an ice cream cone. Another said he remembered that the sky stayed dark for hours that day in the direction of Nagasaki. The Japanese guards' concern was obvious as they stared and pointed in the direction of the blast. George and Max would have witnessed at least a portion of this historic event, since the effects of the blast remained for hours in the western sky and surely would have been the talk of the camp.

With the capture of Okinawa in June 1945, American air crews had steadily increased carpet bombing of the cities on the home islands of Japan, including the capital city of Tokyo itself. WWII veteran, Robert Schneider, who was stationed on Okinawa from July to December 1945, recalled taking a flight to Tokyo shortly after the surrender in August of 1945. He said hardly a building was standing in the city, but that the American bombers were careful not to bomb the emperor's palace, which remained undamaged. By sparing the emperor, it was hoped that

Brothers Born of Adversity

it would be easier to negotiate a surrender. On August 14, 1945, the Japanese Emperor Hirohito agreed to a complete surrender with the condition that it would allow him to maintain his position, although it would become more of a ceremonial role. On September 2, 1945, the Japanese foreign minister signed a treaty of surrender with General MacArthur aboard the USS *Missouri* in Tokyo Bay.

National Archive photo showing mushroom cloud from the atomic bomb dropped on Nagasaki.

The day after the Japanese emperor agreed to surrender, trucks pulled into Camp #17 and Japanese soldiers dismantled and loaded the machine guns and anti-aircraft weapons and removed them from the camp. A little later, more trucks arrived and all of the guards with their

115

packs were loaded on to trucks and driven off. No more Japanese guards would be seen in the camp and two of the American POWs had taken over guard duty at the main gate. The prisoners quickly realized that the war must be over. The next day, on August 16, 1945, the men were called to the parade ground in the camp. The American commanding officer who was now in charge of the camp escorted the former Japanese Camp Commandant to the parade ground. Standing on a box, the former Japanese Camp Commandant told the men that the war was now over and that the POWs would soon be taken back to their homelands. He also wished the men well and then was escorted off the parade ground by the American officer. It was an emotional moment and some men cried. The war was finally over. They had survived so much. Many were shouting for joy and others were thanking Jesus and praising God for their deliverance.

The men, now realizing that it could be days or weeks before they might be found, made a big PW sign on the parade ground using white shells to let the American pilots flying overhead know that the compound contained prisoners of war. Some men had managed to keep their countries' flags hidden while imprisoned, but now started putting them up on the camp fence. A squadron of planes flying over noticed the sign and flew back over, coming down low to let the men that were waving below know that they had been spotted. The next day a transport plane flew over the camp and dropped a parachute dispatch which advised the men that their position had been reported and that food and medical supplies would soon be dropped. It also advised them to stay clear of the drop area since the canisters would sometimes break open creating a hazard to those below.

Food and medicine were soon being delivered by air drops from American aircraft to the excitement of the men on the ground. Another dispatch drop was also made that contained a map and a letter that stated, *"If you look at the map you will note that this area was to be completely obliterated in a bombing raid set for 15th August."* George and Max and their fellow POWs would have had to wonder how many times they had escaped death since their captivity.

After the canisters fell to the ground, men eagerly started sorting through the items, discovering food items that they hadn't tasted in years. As the earlier dispatch had warned, some of the canisters broke open in midair. One man eager to retrieve items had his foot badly damaged by a falling can of peaches. A Japanese woman living near the camp, who survived the air raids, was killed by a case of pork and beans as she walked out the door of her house. Some bottles of medicine had broken or lost their lids during the drop, spilling pills on the ground, making it difficult to identify what they were. This situation was made worse because the medical staff could not recognize the names of many of the medicines. The medical staff was simply out of touch with some of the newer medicines being used at the time. A dietitian was parachuted into the camp to advise the recovering men on what foods they should be eating. As the days passed, the men were quickly starting to gain some of their weight back.

National Archive photo of General Douglas MacArthur witnessing the signing of documents of surrender by the Japanese foreign minister aboard the USS *Missouri* in Tokyo Bay on September 2, 1945.

On September 2, 1945, the gates of the camp were opened and a car full of American officers pulled up outside. The officers advised the men

Brothers Born of Adversity

that Japan had surrendered after the United States had dropped atomic bombs on the cities of Hiroshima and Nagasaki. They said that loads of leaflets were distributed over Tokyo warning the Japanese to surrender before those bombs were dropped. The officers tried to answer questions the men were shouting out. There were so many things the men wanted to know after being imprisoned for so long.

Some of the men searched the mines for the Japanese and Formosan overseers who had abused them during their imprisonment. It was now payback time if they could find them. Men started exploring the surrounding area outside the camp and looking for souvenirs. Some found a large quantity of Red Cross supplies that had been received a year or two earlier that were never distributed to the men. They also discovered and helped rescue some nearly starved Chinese POWs who were in a nearby camp and had been used as laborers in the coal mines as well. The American POWs had not been aware of their existence.

Despite the food and medicine from the air drops, deaths were still occurring in the camp from the diseases and malnutrition that they had endured. Reporter George Weller visited the camp several times, interviewing many of the men, including Max. Hearing the tales from the men who survived the voyage on the *Oryoku Maru*, *Enoura Maru*, and *Brazil Maru*, the reporter recognized the historical significance and wrote a series of articles about the hell ship voyages for the Chicago Daily. He later wrote his book, *First into Nagasaki*, about their experiences. One interesting comment he recorded in his book came from an officer who survived the hell ship voyage. Reflecting upon accounts from the men about how horrific the Japanese were, this officer said that he and his fellow survivors were devils as well, or they would not have survived. He went on to say that the generous, brave, and unselfish men were those who were left behind. While he may have been projecting his own actions on all of the rest of the survivors, it might be easy to understand how a starving POW might take more than his share of food and water or commit worse deeds in order to survive.

George and Max recognized September 13, 1945, as their day of liberation, presumably when the camp was secured by the Allied military forces. Two days later on September 15th, they would pass through the gates of the prison camp for the last time. From the camp, the now former POWs were transported to the Omuta railway station where they boarded a train and took the long horseshoe loop around the bay and on to the Nagasaki peninsula. Entering the Nagasaki area, the train moved slowly along, allowing the men to get a view of the devastation of the city, which showed no sign of life. Robert Holman, in his book *On Paths of Ash*, described the air as full of a pungent odor as from a crematorium chimney, and said that human skeletal remains could be seen along the train's route.

Once they arrived at the station, they found it swarming with American naval officers, doctors, nurses, welfare workers, Red Cross workers, and other personnel. Also lined up seeking aid were many Japanese citizens with horrific atomic ash injuries waiting to be treated. The former POWs were directed to a prefab building that had been erected with showers, decontamination areas, and a field dressing area. There the men were directed to remove their clothing, walk forward under showers, dusted with a powder, which was probably DDT, checked with a Geiger counter, and fitted with American enlisted men uniforms and caps. Then they were served coffee and donuts by some of the first Caucasian women that they had seen in years.

Stretcher cases of former POWs from Camp #17 arriving in Nagasaki, Japan by train. Public domain photo.

Brothers Born of Adversity

In the harbor awaiting them was a fleet of ships waiting to evacuate the ex-POWs from Japan, which some referred to as the "Magic Carpet" fleet. Among this fleet was a destroyer named the USS *Smith*, which would evacuate Max and George. Patrol boats took the men out to the waiting fleet where they would be treated well and made comfortable. As the ships pulled out of the harbor, many of the men watched as Japan faded out of sight. It was probably all so surreal for George and Max who had been prisoners for so long. They had been shot at, slapped, beaten, nearly suffocated, survived the bombing of their "hell ships", as well as the torpedoes; nearly died from thirst, lack of food, excessive heat and frigid temperatures, and disease. They witnessed the death and murder of friends and comrades, and some of the worst in human cruelty -- yet, somehow, they survived.

Now George and Max were safe, with plenty of food and drink, clean clothes, and caring people offering them comforts and entertainment. Then, as if some dark force was not through with them, they endured the violent winds, rain, and waves of a typhoon before they reached Okinawa. As the USS *Smith* approached the island and awaited an opportunity to dock, George and Max witnessed the largest armada of naval ships ever assembled in any single place in the history of the world.

At Okinawa, George, Max, and the other Allied POWs were processed through a transient camp for former POWs where they would be questioned about their prison experiences. There, to George's amazement, were two of his sisters, Thelma and Aller, who met him the moment he arrived at the transient camp. By this time, Aller was a Captain and Thelma a Lieutenant. They both now outranked their brother! With the aid of the Red Cross Recovered Personnel Locator Service, they knew where George would be processed and they were there to meet him as he arrived. George's initial reaction was sheer astonishment to see his sisters, but it quickly turned to kisses and embraces. It had been years since he had seen his sisters, and now two of them were there in army nurse's uniforms embracing him. After introducing Max, George was anxious to know about his parents and other sisters. The reunion drew the attention of those around them, including an American Red Cross photographer who captured this endearing moment in the photo that follows. This photograph was later published in newspapers back home in the States.

After heartfelt hugs and greetings and a brief update about family back home, Thelma and Aller insisted on buying something for George from the base store. Without much thought, George asked for nail clippers. Of everything George could have asked for, like cigarettes, a cold beer, clothes, or food, he chose nail clippers. Sometimes it's the simplest of things in life that we take for granted that matter most.

Although George was elated to see and catch up with his sisters, he now wanted to focus on getting back home to Alabama and seeing the rest of his family. Max had heard so many stories about George's family during their years of imprisonment that they may have seemed like family to him as well. He was now focused on seeing his mother and putting the war behind him. He too had his sights set on home.

Brothers Born of Adversity

"Okinawa, Sept. 1945 – C. Ph. M. George Crowell, a former prisoner of the Japanese is reunited with his sisters, Capt. Aller Crowell, left, and Lt. Thelma Crowell, army nurses from Berry, Alabama, who appealed to the American Red Cross recovered personnel locator service to help find their brother. They located him the moment he arrived at the Okinawa transient camp. (American Red Cross photo by Hamlin) E879."

Brothers Born of Adversity

Epilogue

The end of the war brought freedom for thousands of former POWs and the opportunity for many GIs to return home to families and restart their lives. For Japan, it would mean seven years of occupation by Allied forces. Many of the Japanese military personnel would be tried for their war crimes. Appendix A provides some of the specific charges and judgements against those involved in the murders and brutal treatment of the POWs who were transported on the *Oryoku Maru*, *Enoura Maru*, and the *Brazil Maru*.

One of the most immediate issues that the Allied occupation forces had to address was the critical food shortages of the Japanese people. Significant aid had to be provided to prevent thousands of Japanese citizens from starving to death.

While there was a desire to punish Japan for starting the war in the Pacific, there was also an interest in seeing Japan successfully rebuild, become a democracy, and a future ally. General MacArthur was chosen to oversee the occupation and insisted upon allowing Emperor Hirohito to remain on the Imperial Throne. Having Hirohito remaining in his palace, although in a much more limited role than in the past, made it much easier for MacArthur to successfully meet the goals of the occupation forces. Hirohito was pressured into announcing to the Japanese people that he was not divine, and that the Japanese were not in fact superior to other races or destined to rule the world.

During the war period, both the Americans and Japanese portrayed each other in art and posters in the worst possible way. It is a tribute to those in leadership positions in the decades after the war, that both Japan and the United States could put off the deep bitterness that each side had felt for each other during the war and become friends and brothers among the nations.

With the end of WWII, China renewed its civil war, with the communists eventually taking control over the Chinese mainland and the nationalist forces fleeing to Taiwan. With the Chinese embroiled in a civil war, neither side was pushing for retribution against the Japanese for the

Brothers Born of Adversity

atrocities they had committed against the Chinese people. Both sides thought it was better for their own self-interest to develop good relations with the island nation, which they knew would again become a major power in the area. Unlike the Japanese mainland, the occupation of Korea was partitioned, with Russia occupying the North and the United States the South, divided by the 38th Parallel. This would eventually be the cause of much U.S. concern as tensions grew between the North and South Koreas, and eventually resulted in the Korean War.

Yet for others, they would see an opportunity for new business interests in the occupation and rebuilding of Japan. One such individual was Ted Lewin. Once he had the opportunity, he moved to Tokyo and set up legal as well as illicit operations similar to what he had in Manila. He would be very successful there for a time but would eventually be deported by the Japanese. At which point he returned to Manila and reestablished his former operations there.

With the end of WWII, most GIs and former POWs were simply interested in putting the war behind them and getting on with their lives, and George and Max were no exceptions. By October 1945, George and Max had arrived back in California where they would undergo evaluation and any treatment they might need as a result of their experiences as POWs. The following month the men were transferred to Memphis, Tennessee. Then on December 7, 1945, four years to the day from the start of war in the Pacific, George and Max were granted three months rehabilitative leave. Neither man could hardly wait to get back home to his family. It had been over six years since either one had been home.

In Berry, Alabama, George's mother, father, his younger sisters, and other family members and friends anxiously awaited George's return. In Birmingham, Alabama, Max's mother, family, and friends couldn't wait to see him as well. While time and the war experience had certainly aged both George and Max, there had been changes among both men's families. The most apparent ones were in George's family. George's maternal grandfather, Daniel Dunn, had passed away during the years George had been imprisoned. His parents had aged, but it was much more visible in George's father. His health had begun declining from the

Brothers Born of Adversity

years of hard work, the stress of providing for his family, and wondering if he would see his son and daughters again.

George's sister, Gene, who was a teenager the last time George had been home, was now serving as an army nurse in Europe. George's two remaining younger sisters, Willie Nell and Billie Dove, who were 15 and 11 years old the last time he was home were now young women age 21 and 17, respectively. It must have been a heartwarming homecoming for both George and Max. Family members remember George hugging his father affectionately and then, to everyone's amusement, heard George thank his father for all those whippings he got as a child growing up. He said it sure helped prepare him for what he was to experience while imprisoned by the Japanese.

During their years of imprisonment together, George often told Max that after the war he wanted him to come visit in Berry and meet his five beautiful sisters. Max had already met two of the sisters, Thelma and Aller, in Okinawa, shortly after their liberation. Soon after returning home Max made a trip to visit George in Berry. As it worked out, Max and George's sister, Willie Nell, took an immediate liking to one another and within a year were married. While George and Max may have felt like they had become as close as brothers through the adversity that they had experienced together, they would now be true brothers, or at least brothers-in-law. Over their years of imprisonment, beatings, and near-death experiences together George and Max had formed a bond of friendship that few people experience. Both men had provided help and encouragement to each other when needed most and their bond of friendship endured the rest of their lives.

George and Max received Purple Hearts and several other military medals for their service in the war. Several years after the war, Max was nominated for and received the Bronze Star Medal for his service and commitment to his fellow POWs while on the hell ships. The corresponding citation reads in part as follows, "...Maxwell made every effort possible to alleviate the suffering of his fellow prisoners and sustain their morale, despite his own intense suffering. With conditions rapidly becoming more acute as the prisoner of war draft was forced to transfer to an unsanitary cattle boat following the sinking of the Oryoku Maru on

Brothers Born of Adversity

December 15, he labored unceasingly to aid the men dying from suffocation and from wounds sustained as attacks continued unabated. When his vessel was again bombed on January 9, he aided in evacuating the sick, wounded and half-starved survivors to a third prison ship, where he voluntarily stood daily regular watches as long as his waning strength permitted, continuing to care for patients, control all available sanitary measures and identify and properly dispose of the dead until, upon arrival at Moji, the 500 remaining survivors were transferred to Japanese prison camps. Stouthearted and courageous throughout this perilous voyage, Pharmacist Maxwell, by his outstanding and self-sacrificing devotion to his fellow-men, served as an inspiration to all prisoners on board and upheld the highest traditions of the United States Naval Services." Most, if not all of the above could be said about George and the other corpsmen, but it is obvious that Max's performance did stand out and was recognized by his superiors.

George would continue his career in the U.S. Navy until retirement and then work several years in a civil service position. After remaining single for seven years after returning from the war, he finally met a woman he couldn't pass up, Mattie Frances Edwards, from Ellenboro, North Carolina. They married in 1952 and had two children, Georgia Lee and Perry Wyman. Like most military families, they would periodically move to wherever George's next assignment took him. George and Mattie eventually settled in Pensacola, Florida, where they lived the rest of their lives.

George, at least in his later years, was not a very religious man and he found it difficult to forgive the Japanese for the treatment he experienced as a POW. While George had a loving family relationship with his parents and sisters, he left the raising of the children to Mattie and didn't show a strong interest in what the children were doing growing up. He loved his children and always provided for their physical needs, but there was not the closeness with his children that one might expect with him having been raised by a very loving family.

George and Mattie's son, Perry, left home after graduating from high school and attended the University of West Florida and Florida State University. Through hard work and dedication, he earned bachelor's, master's and doctoral degrees. He pursued a career in finance and administration at Florida State University and lives in Tallahassee, Florida with his wife Marilyn. They have two daughters, Casey Lee and Natalie Brooke. George and Mattie's daughter, Georgia, lived in Birmingham, Alabama, and was finishing studies for a second career in real estate when she passed away unexpectedly in 2006.

Wedding photo of George and Mattie Crowell in 1952.

Perry remembers his father not having many close friends, but he was respected by those who knew his military history. He was quiet, not very sociable and avoided crowds and social events, but he always loved times he spent with his parents, sisters, and Max. He maintained a strict work and home routine, smoked non-filtered Lucky Strike cigarettes, drank Falstaff beer, and Early Times was his whiskey of choice. George had his fill of rice while a POW, so that food was something that was never served at home after the war. Like many of the surviving POWs, George started developing health issues early which the doctors believed could have resulted from his contracting beriberi while he was imprisoned. George died unexpectedly in 1982 following surgery when he was 70 years old. He is buried at the Barrancas National Cemetery in Pensacola, Florida.

Brothers Born of Adversity

George's widow, Mattie, remained in Pensacola, where she died in 2003, at age 84, after suffering a fall. Mattie was adamant that when she died her body be given to a medical school for study. Perry ensured that her wishes were carried out.

Pictured below is the front and back of a card George carried in his wallet showing his navy assignments, beginning with his capture in the Philippines. The front portion he called his prison record and the back one his ratings.

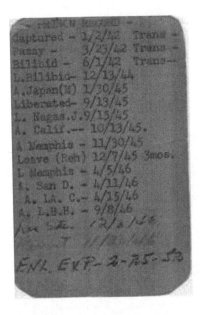 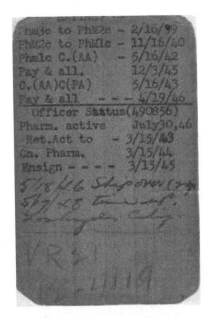

Max continued his career in the U.S. Navy after the war, retiring after 30 years, and then worked for the Florida Health Department. Max and his wife Willie Nell had two children. The family would move about every two years to follow Max's navy career, eventually settling in Jacksonville Beach, Florida.

Max named his son George Gary Maxwell, a tribute to George and their bond of friendship. George Gary followed in his father's footsteps and made a career in the Navy, becoming a pilot after graduating from the United States Naval Academy in Annapolis, Maryland. He retired at the rank of captain. Max and Willie also had a daughter, named Michele, who like her father and aunts had a passion for caring for people, and pursued a career in nursing. Michele remembers her father as being calm, caring, and considerate with his interactions with people. He was well liked and made friends easily and played an active role in his children's lives. His children recall how he always stressed the importance of honesty and integrity, maintaining a good name, and being committed to their Christian faith.

Max and Willie Maxwell's wedding
photo in 1946.

Experiencing the horrors of war and violence can have a way of dehumanizing the enemy and, like a cancer, a hatred can grow for a whole ethnic group. Max's children would recall that their father was able to put off any bitterness toward the Japanese, but for many others, including George, the bitterness would remain.

Max would die of cancer at the age of 60 in 1980, and Willie Nell died of a stroke at the age of 79 in 2003. Max and Willie are both buried at the H. Warren Smith Cemetery in Jacksonville Beach, Florida.

Brothers Born of Adversity

George's older sister, Thelma, never married and made a career out of being an army nurse. After the Korean War started, Thelma spent 17 months in Korea, often close to the front line nursing the many casualties from the fighting. After her father's health declined, Thelma played a key role in supporting her parents. At that time, her parents did not qualify for Social Security, and Medicare and Medicaid did not yet exist, so the care of the parents fell to the children. George was known to have contributed $2,000 to his parents in 1947, nearly the equivalent of $30,000 in today's dollars. Most certainly the other siblings contributed as well.

Thelma died in 1980 at the age of 69, and is buried at Barrancas National Cemetery in Pensacola, Florida, as is her brother George.

George's sister Aller would serve as an army nurse for a total of 10 years, resigning her position after marrying an infantry officer named Quentin L. Humberd on New Year's Day 1949. Quentin was an active-duty Infantry Officer and made a career of his military service, which required moving with his family frequently. Aller and Quentin had two children, Brenda, who like her mother became a nurse, and Quentin Allen, who became a pediatrician and served on active duty in the Army Medical Corps for 13 years, resigning at the rank of Lt. Colonel.

At some point before going to serve in Okinawa, Aller had the opportunity to meet the First Lady, Eleanor Roosevelt, as shown in the following photograph:

Brothers Born of Adversity

Aller Crowell standing next to First Lady, Eleanor Roosevelt.
Photo from family's collection.

Aller lived to be 80 years old and passed away in 1994. She is buried in the Tennessee Veterans Cemetery in Knoxville, Tennessee. Aller's husband Quentin passed away 11 years prior to Aller and chose to be buried next to family in Bradley County, Tennessee.

George's sister Gene, who had also become an army nurse, served in Europe near the end of the war or shortly thereafter. She met and married an army officer named Wythe Parks Brookes who was a Combat Engineer. Gene resigned her position after marrying. They had one son named Peter Crowell Brookes who became an engineer but was tragically killed in a mountain climbing accident on Mount Rainier in Washington State when he was 26 years old. Gene had lost her husband to cancer seven years prior to the death of their son. A few months after her son's death, Gene was diagnosed with cancer and died several months later in July of 1982 at the age of 61. She chose to be buried next to her son at Floral Hills Memory Gardens in Tucker, Georgia. Her husband Wythe served in WWII and Korea. He died at 56 years of age and is buried in the National Cemetery in Chattanooga, Tennessee.

The youngest sister, Billie Dove, did not pursue a career of her own, but was instrumental in the day-to-day care of her parents. After their passing, she would eventually also care for Thelma in her later years as

Brothers Born of Adversity

well as other family members when needed. It is said that she and a man named Garvis, who was also caring for his elderly mother, had committed to marrying each other once their parents had passed away and they were no longer needed to care for them. Unfortunately, Garvis's mother outlived him and as a result the marriage never occurred. Billie died in 1997 at age 69 and is buried next to her parents at the Tuscaloosa Memorial Park in Tuscaloosa, Alabama.

In researching the story of George and Max's imprisonment, it was hard not to wonder what in their background might have helped contribute to their survival, as well as how their later lives were impacted as a result of their war experiences. In Appendix B – Lingering Effects of the POW Experience - an attempt was made to explore these questions. While it seems fairly certain that a strong faith in God, support from loving families, and having a close supportive friendship during the POW experience played a role in their survival, it is not quite so easy to understand how their later lives were impacted. Since neither George nor Max rarely mentioned their war experiences, much of what they endured during the war and the memories that might have haunted them in later life will always remain a mystery. It is a tribute to both men and those with similar experiences that despite the years of abuse they experienced and the horrors they witnessed they were able to live fairly normal lives after the war.

Brothers Born of Adversity

Appendix A – War Crime Trials

After the war, many of the Japanese involved in the mistreatment of the POWs on the *Oryoku Maru, Enoura Maru,* and *Brazil Maru* were tried for war crimes. Public Relations Informational Summary No. 574, issued by the General Headquarters Supreme Commander for the Allied Powers Legal Section, Tokyo, Japan, dated 9 May 1947, subject titled: *Result of the Trial of Junsaburo TOSHINO, et al.,* provides a powerful summary of charges and sentences for the accused and of the related events for which they were being tried. As a result, it seemed reasonable to include the entire summary below. Note that spelling and grammatical errors were not corrected.

"Death by hanging for two: 25, 20 and 10 year imprisonments at hard labor were for four, and the remaining two of the eight defendants were acquitted.   These were the verdicts handed down by the Military Commission hearing in the case against the eight Japanese charged with being concerned in the deaths of more than 1300 prisoners of war being transported from Manila to Moji, Japan, where they were destined to be disposed throughout Japan for use in labor battalions."

"Junsaburo TOSHINO, former Lieutenant and Guard Commandant aboard the "Hell Ship" was found guilty of murdering and supervising the murder of at least 16 men. In other specifications the accused was found guilty of causing the deaths of numerous other prisoners of war. TOSHINO was the first to receive the death sentence, the other was Kazutane AIHARA, Lance Corporal. The prisoners nicknamed him "Air Raid" because every time he came near the prisoners someone would yell "air raid" and all of them would take cover to escape being beaten by AIHARA. He was in charge of the gardening details and other details the prisoners were working on during their stay in Cabanatuan. He was sentenced to hang for killing numerous American Prisoners of War and participating in the decapitation and stabbing of 15 others."

"Shusuke WADA, whose charges paralleled those of TOSHINO, was the official interpreter for the guard group. He was found guilty of causing the deaths of numerous American and Allied Prisoners of War by neglecting to transmit to his superiors requests for adequate quarters, food, drinking

Brothers Born of Adversity

water and medical attention. WADA was sentenced to Life Imprisonment at hard labor."

"Suketoshi TANOUE, Sergeant Major, was found guilty and sentenced to 25 years at hard labor. He was found guilty of the charge and specification charging him with the killing of 15 prisoners of war at the San Fernando Cemetery by decapitation and stabbing."

"Jiro UEDA, Private, was found guilty of the charge and specification and was sentenced to twenty years imprisonment at hard labor. He was also connected with the killing of the 15 prisoners of war at the San Fernando Cemetery."

"Sho HATTOR, Sergeant of the Guard, was found guilty of the charge and specifications four. As Sergeant of the guard he deprived the prisoners of drinking water and failed to restrain Japanese Military personnel subject to his supervision from beating the prisoners. He was sentenced to 10 years imprisonment at hard labor."

"Hisao YOSHIDA, guard, and Risaku HOBAYASHI, medical corpsman, were acquitted. They were charged with being connected in the murder of the 15 sick prisoners of war at San Fernando Cemetery."

"The charges against TOSHINO and WADA are almost parallel. Both are charged with being responsible with the deaths and inhuman treatment received by the prisoners. TOSHINO is charged with failing to provide adequate quarters, food, drinking water and medical attention, and by refusing to provide reasonable measures for the protection of the prisoners from the hazards of war. It was charged that TOSHINO did willfully kill an American Prisoner of War by shooting him. Another charge against the accused was the fact that he ordered and permitted his military subordinates to kill 15 American Prisoners of War by stabbing and shooting at San Fernando, Pampanga, Philippine Islands."

"WADA was charged with refusing to transmit to his superiors requests made by the prisoner commanders and failing to provide adequate quarters, food, drinking water and medical attention."

Brothers Born of Adversity

"The other members in the group of defendants are charged variously with taking part in the decapitation of the 15 Prisoners at San Fernando, Pampanga, and with numerous beatings and other brutalities which occurred during the voyage from Manila to Moji."

"The Oryoku Maru sailed from Manila 13 December 1944. It was bombed by American planes at Subic Bay. The ship was damaged so badly that the prisoners and all other occupants were moved from the ship and interened at Olongapo Naval Base. While there, the prisoners were afforded no sanitary conditions whatsoever. Numerous deaths occurred and prisoners were treated as animals. The group of prisoners were then moved to San Fernando, La Union, from whence they boarded the Enoura Maru and Brazil Maru, both Japanese transport ships which were to take them to Takao, Formosa. The ships arrived at Formosa and while laying in the harbor they were bombed. The Enoura Maru was damaged so badly that all the prisoners were moved onto the Brazil Maru. After several days at Takao, the Brazil Maru sailed for Moji, Japan, arriving on or about 30 January 1945."

"Of the 1619 prisoners who boarded the Oryoku Maru at Manila, approximately 450 survived to disembark at Moji."

"In making a statement on the case, Mr. Alva C. Carpenter, Chief of the Legal Section, General Headquarters, Supreme Commander for the Allied Powers says, "Of all the cases of brutality and mistreatment accorded prisoners of war that have come out of World War II, none can compare with the torment and torture suffered by our soldiers, who were prisoners of war of the Japanese, aboard the ships, Oryoku Maru, Brazil Maru and Enoura Maru on the voyage from Manila to Japan during the months of December 1944 and January 1945. It is a saga of men driven to madness by sadistic and sensual captors. Today, of the 1619 men who set sail on the voyage, less than 200 are alive. I have read diaries, written at the time, tomes of recorded testimony, have talked to survivors, and no place in recorded history can one find anything so gruesome and horrible. No mitigating circumstances can explain or condone such cruelty. The callous and vile conduct of the captors will live in infamy!""

Brothers Born of Adversity

"The prosecutors for this case were Mr. Allan R. Morrison of 4496 Aukai Street, Honolulu, Hawaii: Mr. Tomas D. Aitken of 540 Stockton Street, San Francisco, California and Mr. Leonard Rand of 537 Summer Avenue, Newark, New Jersey."

"There were originally nine defendants in this case. When the Prosecution rested its case, the defense made a motion for the dismissal of the case against Shin KAJIYAMA, the Captain of the Oryoku Maru. The motion was sustained by the Commission on the grounds that it was developed in the course of the trial that there was nothing which KAJIYAMA could have done to have prevented the atrocities. It was brought out during the trial that KAJIYAMA had protested taking the prisoners aboard the ship at the start and continued to protest and was threatened with court-martial if he did not take the prisoners aboard the ship without further argument. The evidence further indicates that he had made several attempts to alleviate the condition of the prisoners but, inasmuch as he was a civilian merchantman in command of a ship chartered by the Army, the group commander refused to let him do anything on behalf of the prisoners. The Court, therefore saw nothing for which he could be held."

"In the fall and winter of 1944, the Japanese High Command had decided to transport all able-bodied prisoners of war captured in the Philippines to Japan for use as slave labor. The case against the eight defendants concerned a specific case in which 1619 prisoners of war were herded aboard the Oryoku Maru, a Japanese ship which was later christened the "Hell Ship". Christened with blood and sweat of hundreds of prisoners of war. The story of the trip of the 1619 prisoners of war was a shocking, gruesome, repulsive and hideous tale. The story that unfolds for the court and world by the Prosecution was a story of large scale suffering, torture, agony, horror, bloodshed, murder and death. It was as Odyssey which began on 13 December 1944 when a group of prisoners variously estimated at between 1619 and 1630 shuffled through the gates of old Bilibid prison in Manila and trudged wearily to the harbor for embarkation on the Oryoku Maru. These prisoners had been rounded up in compliance with a directive to send all able-bodied prisoners to Japan for labor, and it appeared that the test as to whether or not a man was able-bodied as "can-he-walk". Of course, some of these prisoners had to

136

Brothers Born of Adversity

be helped along by their comrades and some of them collapsed beyond the help of their comrades and had to be picked up by trucks – but that did not affect their status of "able-bodies". The Japanese were scraping pretty hard at the bottom of the barrel when they rounded up this gang of "able-bodied: laborers. There were 92 Lieutenant Colonels, 5 commanders, 170 Majors, 14 Lieutenant Commanders, 261 Army and Marine Corps Captains, 36 Naval Lieutenants, 400 Army Lieutenants, 12 JG Naval Lieutenants, 31 Ensigns, 14 Warrant Officers, 357 Army, Navy and Marine Non-Coms, 181 Army, Navy and Marine enlisted personnel below the rank of Non-Com, and 47 civilians. Most of the enlisted men were medical personal (sic), and the largest class of commissioned officers consisted of Chaplains, Medical, and Dental Personnel."

"Those men who did not reach Moji died of suffocation, starvation, dehydration, disease, bombing, shooting, and beheading, and every single death that occurred was caused by or at least contributed to, by the defendants TASHINO (sic) and WADA. The other defendants were involved in only a part of this mass murder."

Several years after the end of the war following the post-war U.S. occupation and the restoration of Japanese sovereignty, the remaining prison sentence for Shusuke Wada was removed by the Japanese government and he was released.

In a separate trial, Asao Fukuhara, camp commandant for Fukuoka Prison Camp #17, was tried and convicted of war crimes and executed.

After the liberation of Fukuoka Prison Camp #17, the War Crimes Office received numerous complaints about the conduct of U.S. Navy Lieutenant Edward N. Little. Dozens of former POWs reported violations of Rules of Land Warfare and Human Decency at Camp #17 where Lieutenant Little was the messing officer. Three main charges and 22 additional specifications were filed against Lieutenant Little. His defense attorney argued that since he was subject to the Articles for the Government of the Navy, he was under an obligation to report offenders to the Japanese while denying ever doing so. After five months of trial, Lieutenant Little was found not guilty and allowed to finish out his navy career, retiring at the rank of Commander.

Brothers Born of Adversity

While there were countless other Japanese soldiers that were guilty of war crimes, there was not the dogged pursuit of these individuals like there was of the former Nazis. The Chinese civil war had restarted with both sides hoping for favor with the Japanese, so there was not a lot of effort put into trying to find and convict those guilty of war crimes during the Japanese occupation of China. Unfortunately, as a result, many Japanese would deny that the atrocities, such as the Nanjing massacre, ever actually occurred.

The United States and her allies became more concerned with the growing threat of the Soviet Union and civil war that was brewing in Korea, and they were now eager to see Japan rebuild and become an ally in the region. The Japanese emperor claimed that he had not been involved in any significant way with the start of the war, that he had been primarily a figurehead, and it seemed beneficial to the allied governments to accept that assertion. Japan would go on to rebuild with the help of the United States and become a world economic power and a close ally with the United States.

Brothers Born of Adversity

Appendix B - Lingering Effects of the POW Experience

A question explored in researching the story of George and Max was how their lives after the war and those of other surviving POWs might have been impacted from the horrific POW experiences they endured. Today, mental health professionals have made people familiar with a condition they term Post-Traumatic Stress Disorder (PTSD), but it wasn't quite as well understood at the end of WWII. Opinions of those writing about the experiences of the POWs and their ability to live normal lives after the war varied. Some examples from our research follow:

In his book, *First into Nagasaki*, George Weller tells of traveling on a ship returning former POWs home from the Japanese prison camps. He commented that, *"Less than three percent of patients aboard showed any serious psychoneurotic effect from an experience which in many cases had seriously harmed their physical health. Their mental attitude, far from requiring coddling or understanding, was found to be self-confident, normal and fully sane. The paradox that Japanese prison life is turning out men unafraid of the post-war world is explained in their common phrase: "If there's anything tougher ahead than three years in a camp under the Japanese... we cannot imagine what that might be." Psychiatrists say that acute collective normalcy among ex-prisoners is due to the fact that psychoneurotics waned away and died...and that others who harbored such inclinations in the United States, where they gain sympathy, threw them off in Japan. In the prison camps all were really alike, and therefore it was useless for an individual to develop his "social protest" because nobody was any better off, and nobody would listen."*

Duane Heisinger, in his book *Father Found*, has some interesting comments from Dr. Patricia Sutker, who had been Chief of Psychology Service at the Veterans Administration Medical Center in New Orleans in the mid-1980s. Her comments offer an interesting profile of former prisoners as a group. She states, *"Aside from coming to an understanding of your private and collective horror, I have learned about your personal and collective strengths. Most of you were raised in rural environments in loving, patriotic families with the constraints of hard work and schooling. Most of you learned to eat what was put on the table and to suffer inconvenience without complaint. Most of you were accustomed to long*

139

Brothers Born of Adversity

hours of work, minimal frills and luxuries and heavy demands to make ends meet. Many of you were affected by the Depression and took on major adult responsibilities as youths to provide money for the family. You were not indulged as children or allowed to run wild. You were obedient to your parents, subject to discipline, and respectful of authority. Those of you who survived are in some measure alive today because of good fortune [circumstances], but aside from that, you are brave, emotionally stable and disciplined. You are loyal to your country, to your friends and family, and to yourself. You are clever and quick thinking. You do not submit your self-esteem, and you keep alive your dreams of America. You also keep alive your anger, your bitterness and your hatred. Inside, you are not without laughter, and in fact you retain an exquisitely entertaining sense of humor. Strong within you is a sense of self-preservation."

In the editor's notes by Peter Thomson in Robert Holman's book, *On Paths of Ash*, he comments that, *"An ex-POW from Queensland related how he had reunions with his mates from the Burma Railway, when they all met up in the wards of the Brisbane psychiatric hospital. Most families of ex-POWs know such stories, for hospitals of one sort or another played a big part in the ensuing years and post-traumatic stress manifested itself in many ways. In one of his notes, Robert Holman describes bouts of 'suppressed aggression' and how he went through a time of wandering around Sidney looking to get into fights. The numbing refuge of alcohol was turned to by many an ex-POW, though not by Robert Holman, as he never allowed it into his life."* It should be noted that Robert Holman was an Australian who served in the Allied Military.

Aller's son, Dr. Quentin Humberd, who served on active duty as an army pediatrician, commented that more recent mental health research on the health impacts of Adverse Childhood Experiences, or ACEs, had been performed on a large cohort of individuals in California that were followed for decades. These ACEs pale in comparison to the stress of being a POW, but they do provide solid brain science around what stress does to the nervous system and its long-term effects. It has been found that the neurological impacts of stress can vary significantly among individuals. Each POW came to their imprisonment with a unique history of both risk and protective factors that were present from their

140

childhood. For some, the impacts of the severe stress of imprisonment and torture were able to be tolerated and could even strengthen the nature of that person. For others, however, the stress was toxic, and caused both physical and mental changes that endured for the rest of their lives.

The three authors quoted above offer some insightful, but differing perspectives on the lasting effects of the brutality endured by the former POWs, and Dr. Humberd's comments show how these differing perspectives are really connected. It is also worth noting that the United States was better able to fund backpay and pensions than some of the other Allied countries, and also offered assistance such as the G.I. Bill, which allowed many returning service men and women access to higher education. Having meaningful jobs and educational opportunities could have certainly played some part in adjusting back into civilian life.

We can't know what mental and emotional scars men like George and Max might have carried with them the rest of their lives, or how often they might have had nightmares in which they relived some of their worst experiences, or had flair ups of anger for little or no apparent reason. Max's children would say that their father rarely spoke of his POW experiences, other than to say that what happened was so sad. Likewise, George's son Perry said his father rarely talked about his war experience. On the rare occasions that he did, it was not a pleasant experience to behold. For example, Perry recalled how upset his father got watching a CBS evening news report about POWs during the Vietnam War who complained about not being given enough exercise time as required by the Geneva Convention. Of course, his anger was not directed at the POWs being held by the Vietnamese, but the report simply triggered his suppressed anger and rage over the way he and his fellow POWs had been treated by the Japanese. Max, on the other hand, seemed better able to forgive his Japanese captors, which he credited to his strong Christian faith.

George and Max both had successful military careers after their liberation and both married and had families. Both men had issues with alcohol use to some degree, but not to the extent that it affected their careers. George was 40 years old when he finally married and had two

Brothers Born of Adversity

children. George's son, Perry, remembers his father as being quiet, strict, and not very engaged with him or his sister, but never physically abusive to them. It's hard to say whether George's POW experience contributed to that disconnect with his children. On the other hand, George was well respected by others and adored by his sisters. From comments George would make later in life, it was obvious that he was proud of his children and was interested in their future. Max married and had two children as well but had a closer relationship with his children. Although he experienced some problems with alcohol, he overcame them. He credited his strong Christian faith for his ability to overcome the challenges he faced in his life.

While the full extent of how the memories of such horrific experiences affected George and Max later in life is unknown, one can be certain that such memories would not have been easy to forget.

Bibliography
Books and Manuscripts:

1. Geoffrey Pharaoh Adams with Hugh Popham. *No Time for Geishas*, 1973. Geoffrey Pharaoh Adams was a British Officer imprisoned as a POW in Fukuoka Camp #17 from June 1944 to April 1945. He provides one of the most detailed accounts of the conditions and abuses that occurred at the prison camp where George and Max were held in Japan.

2. Charles M. Brown, Lt. Col. AUS Ret. *The Oryoku Maru Story*, an unpublished manuscript. This manuscript was prepared by Lt. Col. Brown from information compiled by four survivors of the *Oryoku Maru*. The manuscript had been sent to George Crowell's family after his death by Ernest Irvin and included some handwritten notes he and possibly others had made regarding imprisonment in Bilibid and the hell ships. Ernest Irvin noted that he remembered George from their imprisonment time together at Bilibid.

3. Charles River Editors. *The Bataan Death March – Life and Death in the Philippines During World War II*, 2020.

4. Sally Mott Freeman. *The Jersey Brothers – A Missing Naval Officer in the Pacific and His Family's Quest to Bring Him Home*, published by Simon & Schuster, 2017.

5. Colonel Nicoll F. Galbraith, GSC, U.S. Army. *Valley of the Shadow: An Account of American POWs of the Japanese*, published by Xlibris, 2018.

6. Duane Heisinger. *Father Found: Life and Death as a Prisoner of the Japanese in World War II*, published by Xulon Press, 2003. Some suggest that this may be the very best documented account of POW prison life in the Philippines and the hell ship experience.

7. Robert Holman edited by Peter Thomson. *On Paths of Ash: The Extraordinary Story of an Australian Prisoner of War*, 2009. Robert Holman was an Australian POW who had been imprisoned at several camps on the Asian continent before being transferred to Fukuoka Camp #17. He devotes just one chapter to his imprisonment in Japan at Camp #17. His account is not as detailed as that of Geoffrey Adams, but provides more details of working in the coal mine and on their liberation.

8. Liz Irvine. *Surviving the Rising Sun – My Family's Years in a Japanese POW camp*, 2010.

9. Christopher L. Kolakowski. *Last Stand on Bataan: The Defense of the Philippines, December 1941 – May 1942,* published by McFarland & Company, Inc., 2016.

10. Manny Lawton. *Some Survived: An Epic Account of Japanese Captivity During World War II,* 1984. Manny Lawton was a hell ship survivor.

11. Robert Mullauer and Raymond A. Dewberry, Ph.D. *Claude Albert Dewberry: A history of his World War II experiences as a captured American prisoner-of-war by the Japanese in 1941. He survived years of death marches, torture, brutality, and starvation until killed in 1945. The Philippine POW story is an epic saga of human endurance. Death was observed at least daily, but often hourly.* Reproduced from the *Dewberry Family of America,* Chapter 17. Copy provided courtesy of the National American Defenders of Bataan and Corregidor Museum and Research Center.

12. Colonel E. B. Miller. *Bataan Uncensored – The True Story of the Death March and the Subsequent Horrors of the Japanese Prison Camps.* First published by Hart Publications, Inc. 1949. Republished in 2018.

13. Davida Michaels MSN, M.Ed., RN. *History of American Nurses World War II.* An article from American Nursing History website dated August 9, 2019.

14. Judith L. Pearson. *Belly of the Beast – A POW's Inspiring True Story of Faith, Courage, and Survival Aboard the Infamous WWII Japanese Hell Ship Oryoku Maru,* published by New American Library, 2001. This book tells of the experience of Pharmacist's Mate Second Class Estel Myers, which closely parallels the experiences of George and Max. Both George and Max were corpsmen like Estel Myers, and they all shared the Bilibid Prison and the hell ship experiences. However, once they arrived in Japan, Estel Myers was placed in a different prison camp than George and Max.

15. G. Kurt Piehler. *A Religious History of the American GI in World War II,* published by the University of Nebraska Press, 2021.

16. Alistair Urquhart. *The Forgotten Highlander – My Incredible Story of Survival During the War in the Far East,* published by Abacus, 2011.

17. George Weller, edited and with an essay by Anthony Weller. *First Into Nagasaki,* published by Three Rivers Press, 2006. In this book, reporter George Weller recounts how he impersonated a colonel to be one of the first into Nagasaki after the war to witness the devastation from the atomic bomb. He also records comments from many of the soon

to be liberated American POWs, primarily from Fukuoka Camp #17, where George and Max were being held, and included two quotes from Max. While interviewing survivors of the *Oryoku Maru* at Camp #17, Weller recognized the historical importance of the tragic events experienced by the men on what would become known as the *"death ships,"* or the *"hell ships."* In his book, he commits over 60 pages to the horrific events, suffering, and deaths of so many men who were being transported on the *Oryoku Maru*, *Enoura Maru*, and the *Brazil Maru*. George Weller also wrote a series of articles about the death ships which were published shortly after the war in the Chicago Daily. These articles were also very useful in piecing together the story of George and Max.

18. Robert Whiting. *Tokyo Underworld – The Fast Times and Hard Life of an American Gangster in Japan,* published by Pantheon Books, 1999.

Articles and Useful Websites:

1. Michael Hurst MBE, Director, Taiwan POW Camps Memorial Society. *The Story of the Bombing of the Enoura Maru*, on-line articles posted by POWTaiwan.org.

2. Roger Mansell website titled, *Center for Research: Allied POWS Under the Japanese,* with Wes Injerd currently in charge of this website. This is a comprehensive website linking numerous documents, photos, and other websites, including the following:
   - Website titled, *WWII Japanese POW Camp Fukuoka #17: History, Rosters and Accounts, Information and Photos of One of the Largest Japanese POW Camps of WWII*, which contains links to a number of other useful websites, documents, photos, etc. This website maintained by Linda Dahl Weeks.
   - Website titled, *POW Research Network, Japan.* Contains information on POW camps. An objective of this network/website includes, *"to know the facts correctly, and hand them down to the people, especially to the young ones, and to talk about them with the former enemies beyond the barrier of the nationalities to enhance mutual understanding, and further to think together about the ways in which we will be able to prevent a recurrence of such tragedies in the past."*
   - Document titled, *Interned by the Japanese in the Philippines,* prepared by Office of the Provost Marshal General, 19 November

1945, and which contains vital information on the POW camps in the Philippines during WWII.

- *Gibbs Report – Fukuoka Camp #17*, by John M. Gibbs, 1946. Contains relevant information on personnel, food, supplies, etc. in Fukuoka Camp #17 during WWII.
- *The Hewlett Report – Fukuoka Camp #17, Omuta, Japan,* prepared by Dr. Thomas H. Hewlett. Contains information on the health and medical conditions within Fukuoka Camp #17. Dr. Hewlett was one of the medical staff imprisoned in Fukuoka Camp #17.

3. *Omuta & its Mafia – just when you thought you have read the worst story!* On-line article posted by 2/4th Machine Gun Battalion, discussing abuses within Fukuoka Camp #17 at Omuta.
4. Lee A. Gladwin. *American POWs on Japanese Ships Take a Voyage into Hell.* A U.S. National Archives and Records Administration article, published in Winter 2003.
5. *The General Courts Martial of Lieutenant Commander Edward N. Little,* posted by William Green, November 13, 2018, on the Blog of the Textual Records Division at the National Archives.
6. *Diary of Lt. David Nash, U.S.A.*, found near former POW camp No. 1, near Cabu, Feb. 5, 1945. Courtesy of the National American Defenders of Bataan and Corregidor Museum and Research Center.
7. Gilbert King. *Minter's Ring: The Story of One World War II POW.* August, 2011, article in Smithsonian Magazine.
8. Wikipedia was found to be useful in obtaining general information on events, locations, ships, individuals, etc.

Other Sources

1. George Crowell's military records, which were obtained with the assistance of Senator Marco Rubio's office.
2. *Detailed engagement report of Oryoku Maru.* Courtesy of the National American Defenders of Bataan and Corregidor Museum and Research Center.
3. Biography of Captain Albert E. Durie, Jr. who died on the *Brazil Maru,* written by his daughter Ann Durie Westerfield. Included with this short biography was a copy of the last letter Captain Durie sent home to his wife before capture, as well as a letter from Frank G. Jonelis, who served with Captain Durie on Corregidor. Mr. Jonelis' letter

provides details of their service activity while assigned to Corregidor up unto its surrender. Courtesy of the National American Defenders of Bataan and Corregidor Museum and Research Center.

4. Conversations with WWII veteran, Robert Schneider, of Sun City West, Arizona.
5. Crowell and Maxwell family recollections, documents, and pictures relative to George and Max's lives.
6. Public domain photos and maps. Wherever possible an attempt was made to reference the source of photos and maps used, however in some instances the original source was not known.

Brothers Born of Adversity

INDEX

Brothers Born of Adversity

Brothers Born of Adversity

Brothers Born of Adversity

Brothers Born of Adversity